SCHIELE

MARIA COSTANTINO

MAGNA BOOKS

Published by Magna Books
Magna Road
Wigston
Leicester LE18 4ZH

Produced by Bison Books Ltd
Kimbolton House
117A Fulham Road
London SW3 6RL

ISBN 1-85422-642-8

Printed in China

Front jacket: SELF-PORTRAIT AS SAINT SEBASTIAN 1914-15 *(Historisches Museum der Stadt Wien, Vienna)*

Back jacket: NUDE AGAINST A COLORED BACKGROUND, 1911 *(Neue Galerie der Stadt, Graz)*

MARIA COSTANTINO was born in Chicago, Illinois, and studied History of Art, Design, and Film at Sheffield City Polytechnic. She was Film Studies Co-ordinator for Michigan State University, and has lectured at Birkbeck College, University of London, Heatherly School of Art, Chelsea, Barnfield College, Luton, and the American College, London. Her previous books include *Art Nouveau* (1989), *Klimt* (1990), *Leonardo* (1991; co-written with Aileen Reid), *Fashion of the Decades: The 1930s* (1991) and *Frank Lloyd Wright* (1991). Maria Costantino is now based in London, England.

LIST OF PLATES

The Artist's Guardian (Leopold Czihaczek) 9
Madonna and Child 10
Trieste Harbor 11
Sunflower 12
Dead City 13
Portrait of Eduard Kosmak 14
Nude Girl with Crossed Arms (Gerti) 15
Standing Nude Girl 16
Self-Portrait with Black Clay Vase 17
Self-Portrait Pulling Cheek 18
Nude Against a Colored Background 19
Agony 20
Prisoner 22
For My Art and My Loved Ones, I Will Gladly Endure to the End! 23
Wally 24
Portrait of Erich Lederer 25
Self-Portrait with Raised Arms 26
Self-Portrait as Saint Sebastian 27
Two Girls Lying Entwined 28
Death and the Maiden 30
Mother with Two Children 32
Portrait of Edith, Standing 33
Self-Portrait Squatting 34
Edge of Town 35
The Embrace 36
Portrait of Marie Schiele 38
Portrait of Albert Paris von Gütersloh 39
The Family 40
Secession Exhibition poster 42
Woman Sitting with Left Leg Drawn Up 43
Acknowledgments 44

EGON SCHIELE

1890-1918

The names of Egon Schiele and that of his fellow artist, admirer and supporter Gustav Klimt are often linked, yet in fact they represent two completely different tendencies in painting. Where Klimt fused the fluid lines, simplified forms and abstract patterns of *Jugendstil* (German Art Nouveau) into works of decorative splendor, Schiele abandoned ornament and decoration in favor of expressions of anxiety and tension. Like the Norwegian painter Edvard Munch, many of Schiele's pictorial manifestations of angst stemmed from his somewhat traumatic childhood.

Schiele was born on 12 June 1890 in Tulln, a small town on the Danube about 20 miles west of Vienna. At the age of 11 he was sent to live with relatives and went to school in Krems, but a year later he returned to his family, who were now living in Klosterneuburg on the northern outskirts of Vienna. Life for the young Schiele was difficult at home; in January 1905, when he was only 14 years old, his father died of a progressive paralysis believed to have been brought on by the syphilis he had contracted before his marriage. For more than a year, Adolf Schiele, a former station master employed by the Viennese Imperial Railways, had become increasingly physically and mentally ill. By the time he died he was clinically insane. The effect that his father's death had on Egon Schiele was prolonged and profound, and no doubt contributed to the strained relationship between him and his mother. Schiele believed that his mother Maria neglected his father's memory and failed to sympathize with her son's loss, and resented her decision to appoint Leopold Czihaczek, his uncle, as his guardian. Czihaczek was to be the subject of one of Schiele's earliest surviving works, *The Artist's Guardian (Leopold Czihaczek)* (1907), which illustrates Schiele's early talents with its fluid lines and dramatic contrasts of light and dark. In the same year Schiele produced six portraits of his uncle, and while the paintings are startling in their analytical visual perception, they show little or no real affection for the sitter. His mother's decision to send her son to live with an uncle with whom he had little in common compounded Schiele's sense of personal tragedy and grief.

At high school in Klosterneuberg Schiele had been taught and encouraged by a sympathetic teacher, Ludwig Karl Strauch, who suggested, against the wishes of Schiele's mother and uncle, that he should apply to art school in Vienna. In 1906 Schiele submitted some drawings and an early portrait of Czihaczek to the Kunstgeweberschule. These were sufficiently impressive that he was advised to apply to the more prestigious, yet more traditional, Academy of Fine Arts in Vienna. Schiele passed the entrance examination and his formal artistic training began. For the first year he drew from plaster casts of the human body and studied academic art history. Only then were students allowed to progress to life drawing classes.

It appears that Schiele initially responded well to the formal artistic training of the Academy but before long he began to clash with his painting tutor Professor Christian Griepenkerl. Griepenkerl was reported to have shouted at Schiele "God has shat you into my class-room," and demanded "For God's sake don't tell anyone that I was your teacher!" Schiele for his part considered his teachers to be "louts" and perpetual enemies, who failed to understand him. The tensions between teachers and pupil were no doubt heightened by the artistic climate in Vienna at the time. In 1898 a breakaway group of radical artists had formed the Austrian Association of Visual Artists, better known as the Vienna Secession, which sought to provide alternative means for exhibiting their works in public. This was in response to the virtual monopoly – some would say stranglehold – of artistic life in Vienna exercised by the Genossenschaft Bildender Künstler (Association of Visual Artists) which had formed in 1861 and had the only large, public exhibition space in the city. Unofficially but effectively allied with the Association was the Academy of Fine Arts, an alliance which added to the conservative "conspiracy" in Vienna at the end of the nineteenth century and foiled any opportunity for the exhibition of avant-garde art. The Vienna Secession intended both to shock the establishment and to educate the Viennese public, who were largely unaware of artistic developments in France, England or the Low Countries. Such artistic insularity meant that few Viennese had ever heard of Manet, Gauguin or Van Gogh!

The first Secession Exhibition, in March 1898, was held at the premises of the Vienna Horticultural Society and included works by Böcklin, Rodin, Carrière, Whistler, Mucha, Knopff and Walter Crane as well as works by the Austrian members. The exhibition was a success on two counts: firstly because the contact with foreign artists contributed significantly to Austrian art; and secondly because it provided an impetus for the plans for a Secession building, to be designed by Josef Maria Olbrich.

In spite, or perhaps because, of the variety of international and national artists whose works were shown at the Secession exhibitions, Schiele's tutor Griepenkerl actively discouraged his students from visiting the Secession. This attitude no doubt made the shows more attractive to curious young artists, who were increasingly bored with the routine of academy art and training.

Reflected in Schiele's work in his early years is his exposure to contemporary painting by artists like Ferdinand Hodler, Edvard Munch and, particularly, Georges Minne, whose attenuated bodies were to play an important role in Schiele's art after 1909. Initially, however, it is the influence of the Post-Impressionists, notably Van Gogh, that is most strongly felt. Compositionally and thematically, Schiele's *Trieste Harbor* (1907) echoes Van Gogh's work at Saintes Maries-Sur-Mer. Likewise the series of paintings of sunflowers, begun in 1907 and continuing occasionally up to 1917, also stem from Schiele's appreciation of Van Gogh, although more in terms of theme than style. Schiele used the motif of sunflowers as emblems in his theme of the life cycle, with its connotations of decay and death, a theme that is central to many of his allegorical paintings. Another early example, *Madonna and Child* (1906-08) with its strange hypnotized faces, is reminiscent of Ferdinand Knopff's paintings of his sister Marguerite, while in style and subject-matter this painting again anticipates later concerns in Schiele's art, the theme of the life cycle which ultimately culminates in death.

It was undoubtedly Gustav Klimt, the leading painter of his generation, founder member and first president of the Vienna Secession, who was to have the most influence on Schiele. It was Klimt who introduced Schiele to more advanced artistic circles, including the Wiener Werkstätte, an offshoot of the Secession which Klimt had joined in 1905. Two of Schiele's paintings in particular, *Watersprites* (1907) and *Danäe* (1907) illustrate Schiele's immediate response to the older artist. These two paintings use specific works by Klimt as starting points in terms of subject matter, style and even title. Nevertheless, in contrast to the decorative and sensual lines of Klimt, Schiele expresses a greater sense of anxiety and threat with his more angular use of line. Similarly, in the *Portrait of Gerti Schiele* (1909), with its use of oil, silver and gold paint, Schiele fuses Klimt's decorative approach with the beginnings of his own more individualistic style. This portrait of his sister has mildly erotic undertones, which are confronted explicitly in the fully nude portrayal *Nude Girl with Crossed Arms (Gerti)* (1910). Schiele's relationship with his sister (like Knopff's relationship with Marguerite) was almost certainly sexual at times. It was during a visit to Trieste with Gerti that Schiele made his first acquaintance with the female body, which was to remain a life-long fascination. In the nude portrayal of Gerti, she stands before the viewer, her arms folded across her breasts in a manner suggesting both vulnerability and embarrassment. Her thin body is over-painted with washes of orange and red watercolor, linking this portrait to Schiele's two self-portraits, *Self-Portrait Pulling Cheek* (1910) and *Self-Portrait Screaming* (1910).

The first self-portrait has been interpreted in terms of Schiele's intense self-awareness and as a parody of his own name – in German "*schielen*" is "to squint," and in the portrait Schiele's eye appears to be doing just that. *Self-Portrait Screaming*, along with *Self-Portrait with Black Clay Vase* (1911), *Self-Portrait Nude, Facing Front* (1910) and *Self-Portrait Masturbating* (1911), are among the earliest and most striking of all Schiele's depictions of "the self" and signal the beginning of a series of works now known as the "radical" portraits. *Self-Portrait Screaming* draws on Expressionist iconography, not least Munch's depiction of *The Scream*. While Munch includes a landscape background, however, Schiele locates himself in an empty space contained by the picture frame. The result is a greater intensity of "sound" together with a heightened sense of alienation and isolation. *Self-Portrait with Black Clay Vase* illustrates Schiele's feelings of vulnerability and confusion: his wide-eyed stare gives him the look of a trapped animal.

In 1909 Schiele left the Academy of Fine Arts, having completed the basic three years of study. He and several like-minded friends formed the Neukunstgruppe (New Art Group) which exhibited at the Pisko Gallery. Although Schiele wrote a manifesto to accompany the show, there was no stylistic theorization, nor were there any plans to remain as a coherent artistic movement. The eclectic group of young and sometimes eccentric men included Anton Peschka (Schiele's future brother-in-law), Anton Faistauer, Erwin Olson and Paris von Gütersloh. Expressionist painter, actor, producer, stage designer and writer, whose first novel *The Dancing Fool* (1910) was one of the earliest examples of Expressionist fiction, Gütersloh was greatly admired by Schiele, who painted the *Portrait of Albert Paris von Gütersloh* (1918) in homage to his friend and fellow artist. This painting was in fact to be Schiele's last oil portrait. Begun in January 1918, it remained unfinished at the time of his death in October.

Schiele's major public debut was to occur not at the Pisko Gallery but at the Internationale Kunstschau in 1908. While the four paintings on show there did not generate an immediate critical response, the very presence of his works in the exhibition opened up new opportunities. By the end of the year Schiele had become acquainted with Arthur Roessler, art critic of the *Arbeiter Zeitung* newspaper, the collectors Carl Reininghaus and Dr Oskar Reichel and the publisher Eduard Kosmak. Schiele was to paint their portraits, but more importantly he received both financial and moral support, particularly from Roessler, who remained a friend and ally throughout Schiele's short life. The *Portrait of Arthur Roessler* (1910) was one of Schiele's earliest commissioned portraits and heralds the emergence of his mature portrait style. Compositionally the portrait reflects the increasingly standardized formula used by Schiele from 1910; the pose and intense expression of the central figure contrast with and are heightened by the austere void-like background. The frontality of the torso, while the head is turned in profile with eyes closed, owes something to the pose adopted by Gerti in Schiele's portrait of his sister from 1909.

The Portrait of Eduard Kosmak (1910) was the last of the 1910 commissioned portraits. Again it uses the square format and again the figure is presented against an empty background, but this time Kosmak confronts the viewer with a rigid frontal pose and a disturbed (and disturbing) stare. (Kosmak was in fact an amateur hypnotist and this probably accounts for the expression on his face.) The pose adopted by Kosmak is also reminiscent of the figure of the young girl in Edvard Munch's painting *Puberty*, a painting which eludes to sexual awakenings. A similar pose can also be seen in Schiele's *Portrait of Poldi Lodzinski* (1910). Here Poldi sits with a white halo above her head, as she smiles out at the viewer with an innocence which is contradicted by her wraithlike arms and aged hands. This portrait was originally made as a study for stained glass windows for the Palais Stoclet in Brussels. Schiele's designs, with the figure of Poldi as the central motif, were ultimately rejected, not because the subject matter was deemed inappropriate, but, ironically for a house that was designed in homage to the International Art Nouveau movement, because the most typically Art Nouveau element in the painting, Poldi's brightly colored blouse, was too bold to be translated into stained glass!

In 1910 the Wiener Werkstätte published three postcards designed by Schiele, and subsequently Josef Hoffmann arranged for him to exhibit with the so-called

"Klimt Group" at the International Hunting Exhibition in Vienna. In the fall, an exhibition in the Klosterneuburg Abbey brought Schiele artistic recognition as well as patronage, in the form of Heinrich Benesch, who soon became the most extensive collector of Schiele's drawings and watercolors. Heinrich Benesch features as one of several surrogate father figures in Schiele's life and was, like Schiele's own father, an official of the Imperial Railway.

The paternalism which Schiele perceived in Benesch is conveyed in *Double Portrait (Otto and Heinrich Benesch)* (1913), in which the older man, large and assured, places a comforting but restraining hand on his son's shoulder. Otto Benesch's wife later commented on the relationship between father and son, and confirmed that Heinrich liked to dominate. Otto Benesch later became a distinguished art historian, Director of the Albertina Collection in Vienna and author of the catalogue introduction for Schiele's first major retrospective show at the Galerie Arnot at the end of 1914. Many have commented on the "cubist" fracturing of the background of this double portrait and relate it to paintings like *Hermits* (1912) and *Agony* (1912), both of which are allegorical double portraits of Schiele and Klimt dressed as monks. The double portrait of Heinrich Benesch and his son is one of the few in which Schiele himself does not feature.

Recognition of Schiele's work gathered pace; by the end of 1912 he had shown at the Galerie Miethke, the Munich Secession, with the Hagenbund, and at the major international Sonderbund Exhibition in Cologne. This rapid and increasingly international success was tempered, at home in Vienna, with a more conservative and even hostile critical reception. Reference was frequently made to Schiele's "grotesque depictions", "ghostly wraiths" and "mutilated corpses." Certainly Schiele's art from 1910 to 1913 gave vent to some of his anger and anguish. His anger was directed at the unresponsive public, which he set out to shock; his anguish was personal, a mixture of intense angst and self-indulgence. Underlying all his work is a preoccupation with the self: in his short career Schiele produced more self-portraits than any other artist, including Rembrandt, and even in his large allegorical compositions Schiele himself appears in various guises.

Schiele's examination of his own sexuality is equally disturbing; standing in front of his studio mirror, he would masturbate while watching himself intently. In the sketches and watercolors which followed, the physical and mental sensations of auto-eroticism are depicted with an unprecedented explicitness, as in *Self-Portrait Nude, Facing Front* (1910) and *Self-Portrait Masturbating* (1911). Until Schiele formed his first lasting heterosexual relationship in the fall of 1911, with Wally Neuzil, a model passed on to him from Klimt, his developing libido seems to have been satisfied (whether because or in spite of his relations with his sister) only through masturbation.

The seventeen-year-old Wally, whose portrait Schiele painted in 1912, was devoted to her lover. In addition to being his model, Wally also undertook most of the household chores and even delivered drawings of herself and other models in erotic poses to various clients. The couple's relationship lasted until 1915, when Schiele returned to his essentially bourgeois roots and decided to make an "advantageous marriage." Wally subsequently left Schiele and served as a nurse in World War I. During the course of her duties, some time in 1917, she was killed.

Underlying many of Schiele's female nude portraits is a sense of sexual pain and repression. Women, and occasionally pre-pubescent girls, are shown as sexual animals and objects of desire. Often the visual focus in the paintings is on their genitalia. *Standing Nude Girl* and *Seated Young Girl* (both 1910) are watercolors which confront the theme of awakening sexuality in pre-pubescent girls. The models, who often came from Vienna's slums, pose unself-consciously and with vacant expressions. Both bodies are tinted with red and green washes which give their skin an aura of disease and decay. While child prostitution was rife in Vienna, and sexually transmitted diseases common in both young and old, Schiele's studies still shocked and outraged many.

In a city of stark contrasts and hypocrisies, pornography flourished, and Schiele relied largely on selling his erotic drawings to provide an income. Despite frequent warnings from friends, Schiele unwisely left many such drawings on open display in his studio, even when children came to pose for him. On 13 April 1912 he was arrested and charged with "immorality" and "seducing a minor." The first charge was upheld and, in addition to a 24-day prison sentence, the presiding judge burnt one of his drawings. The second charge of seduction of a minor relates to a thirteen-year-old girl who, it seems, had simply run away from home and fled to Wally's and

Schiele's house for refuge. Thirteen watercolors, twelve of which are signed and dated, provide an account of Schiele's time in prison. Some sketches are of his cell, some are angst-ridden self-portraits like *Prisoner* (24 April 1912) and *For My Art and My Loved Ones, I Will Gladly Endure to the End* (25 April 1912).

Sex and death were also themes in many of Schiele's large allegorical oil paintings, which were begun in 1910. *Dead Mother* (1910), *Dead Mother I* (1911) and *Dead Mother II* (1911) herald the birth of the series, and contrast the new life in the womb with the gaunt death-like mask face of the mother. Later, after his marriage to Edith Harms in 1915, Schiele was to express the joys of motherhood, but in 1911 the link with pain and suffering is maintained in works such as *Pregnant Woman and Death*. The distinctly melancholic mood even appears in Schiele's paintings of the landscape surrounding Krumau, his mother's home town, where he spent some time between 1910 and 1911; *Houses and Roofs near Krumau* (1911) has an overbearing darkness, while titles such as *Dead City* (1912) convey what Schiele saw as the "destitution of a dying town and landscape."

Following his release from prison, Schiele returned to Vienna with Wally and lived in seclusion, but his determination to fight against hypocritical Viennese society culminated in a major oil, *Cardinal and Nun*, a parody of Klimt's *The Kiss* (itself an icon of Viennese *Jugendstil*). *Cardinal and Nun* presents two religious symbols of Catholic Vienna locked in a sexual embrace. Schiele's sense of martyrdom was developed further in works such as the poster entitled *Self-Portrait as Saint Sebastian* (1914-15), for the retrospective exhibition at the end of 1914 at the Galerie Arnot. Such post-prison dejection worried many of Schiele's friends, who rallied in support. Soon he recovered and returned to portraiture, producing the *Double Portrait (Otto and Heinrich Benesch)* and the decorative *Portrait of Fredericke Maria Beer* (1914).

In 1915 Schiele decided to marry. His chosen bride was Edith Harms, the youngest daughter of a middle-class family, whose father coincidentally was also a railway official. The Harms family lived opposite Schiele's studio, and his courtship of Edith began after he displayed a number of self-portraits in his studio windows in order to attract her attention. The scheme proved so successful that Schiele seemed also to have won the heart of Edith's sister Adele. Any doubts which Schiele might have felt regarding which of the sisters to marry was dispelled when Adele announced her intention to become a nun. On the anniversary of his own parents' wedding, Schiele and Edith were married, with Edith's father Johann Harms as the only witness. Later, in 1916, Schiele produced the *Portrait of Johann Harms*, which showed the now retired man in a contemplative mood and which marked the beginning of a series of "painterly" portraits.

The sense of change from Schiele's old way of life to a new one after his marriage was expressed in two large allegorical oils from 1915. *Death and The Maiden* is essentially a "farewell" portrait to Wally, who kneels before her lover clutching his knees. Schiele himself in turn embraces Wally with some detachment and reserve. *Soaring* (1915), the final major double self-portrait, now lost, depicted Schiele as floating upward and away from his earlier self.

Although he was aware of the horrors of World War I raging around him, Schiele did not himself see active service. Following an initial posting to Prague, he returned to Vienna where he was assigned to guard duties, often escorting Russian prisoners of war. *Portrait of a Russian Officer* (1915) is one of a series of portraits of both Russian and Austrian soldiers. Although the war did curtail his artistic output, its effects were only marginal; at least eight oil paintings date from 1916, while in 1917 Schiele produced thirteen oils and numerous watercolors and sketches. Edith, very much in love, followed her husband on his postings, and Schiele's *Portrait of Edith, Standing* (1915) depicts her as an innocent, still virginal, young bride. Painted two months after their marriage, the rigidity of Edith's pose conveys something of Schiele's sexual frustration in the early months of their marriage. This idea is enhanced by the series of three double portraits entitled *Embrace*, in which the tone gradually changes from one of gentle persuasion on Schiele's part to one of mutual ecstatic abandonment.

Schiele's increasing contentment with his marriage finds its fullest expression in his last major allegorical oil, *The Family* (1918), which heralded the announcement of Edith's pregnancy in the spring of 1918 (but which was tragically terminated by her death in October 1918). While it is said that paintings like *The Family* and even the earlier *Mother with two Children* (1915) demonstrate Schiele's own personal transformation into an increasingly mature and secure man, it should be said that he still needed, and apparently found, sexual fulfilment outside his marriage. This was with his models, as the erotic *Reclining Woman* (1917) suggests, although the shocking nature of many of his earlier nude female portraits has been radically tempered.

The last major oil painting on the theme of the family was *The Artist's Wife* which, although signed and dated 1918, was in fact painted in the early months of 1917. Compared to the earlier *Portrait of Edith Standing*, this relaxed depiction helps to suggest a greater marital harmony between the couple. The painting also illustrates Schiele's gradual interest in form rather than in content.

In March 1918, Schiele was invited to take part in the 49th Secession Exhibition. Nineteen oils and 29 drawings were shown, and many were sold at prices previously unknown for his work. Schiele's *Secession Exhibition Poster* (1918) is his version of a Last Supper, with himself at the head of the table. The allusion to Christ is a reminder of Schiele's ego-centric character, but there is also a tender aspect to this image. At the foot of the table is an empty chair, the chair that would have been occupied by Gustav Klimt, who had died in February 1918 of influenza.

The influenza epidemic which ravaged Europe in 1918 was responsible for nearly as many deaths as were the hostilities during World War I. The virus which had claimed the lives of both Klimt and Edith finally struck Schiele. Three days after his wife, on 31 October 1918, he died.

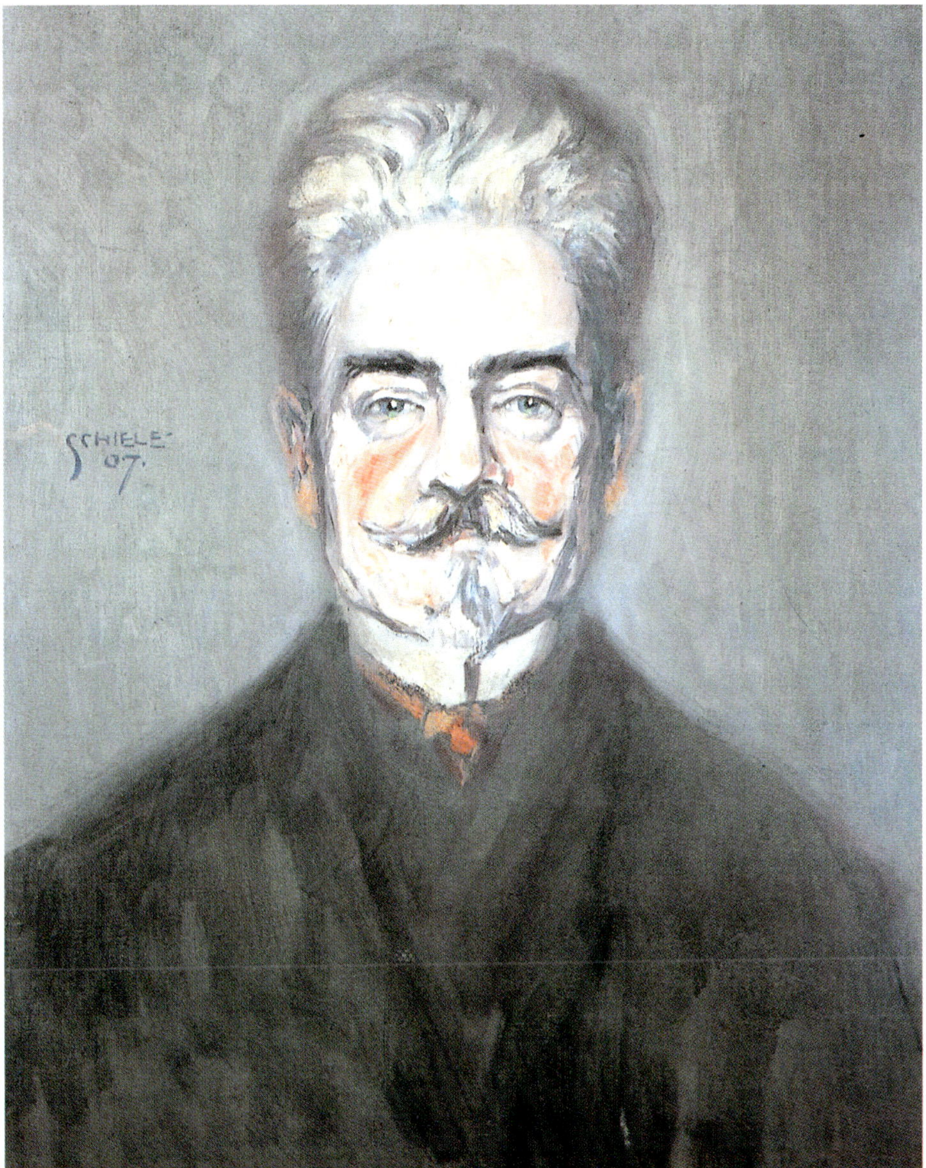

THE ARTIST'S GUARDIAN (LEOPOLD CZIHACZEK), 1907
Oil on canvas, 24⅝ × 18¾ inches (62.7 × 47.2 cm)
Private Collection

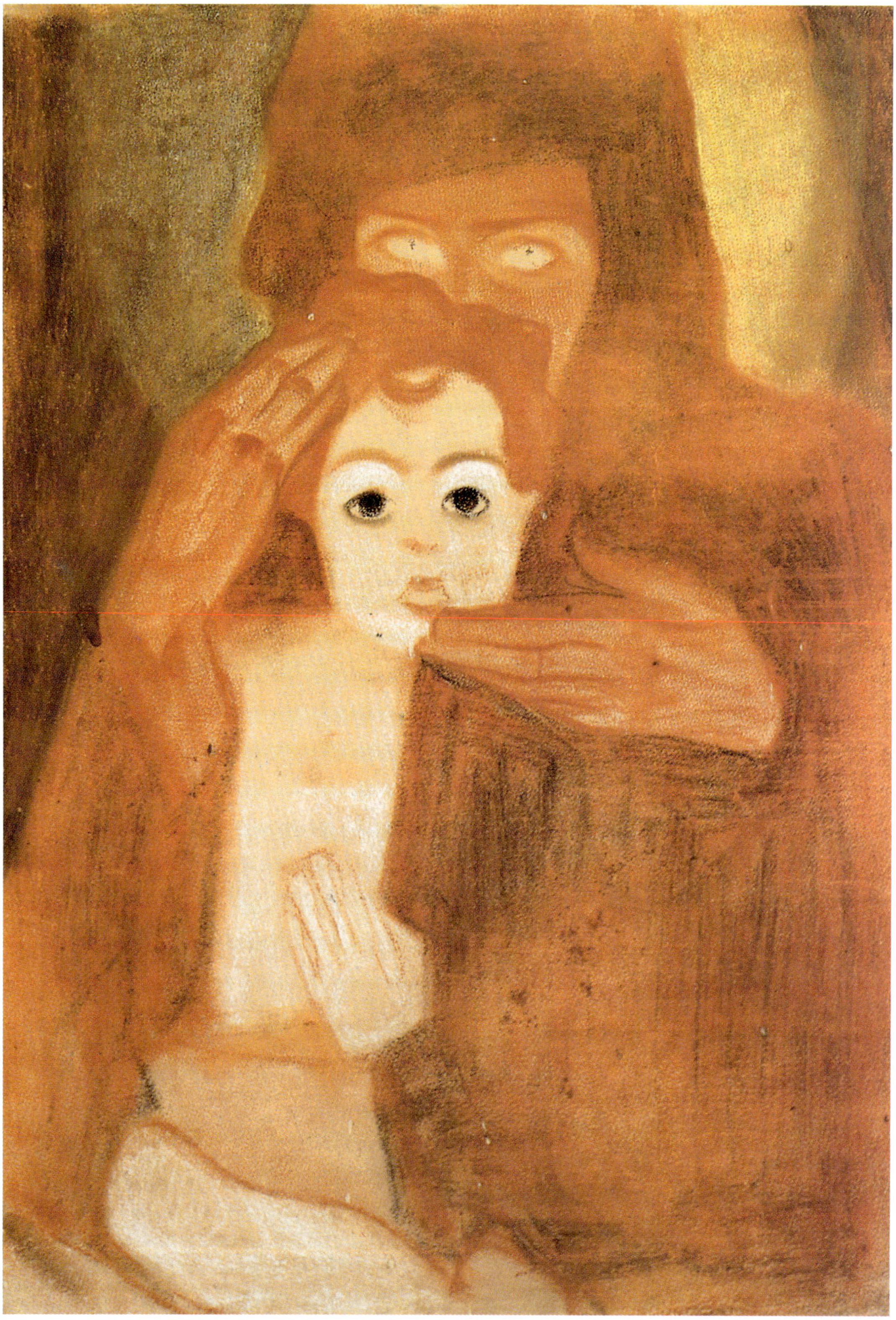

Above:
MADONNA AND CHILD, 1906-08
Colored chalks, 23½ × 17 inches (60 × 43.5 cm)
Niederösterreichisches Landesmuseum, Vienna

Right:
TRIESTE HARBOR, 1907
Oil on cardboard, 9¾ × 7¼ inches (25 × 18 cm)
Neue Galerie am Landesmuseum Joanneum, Graz

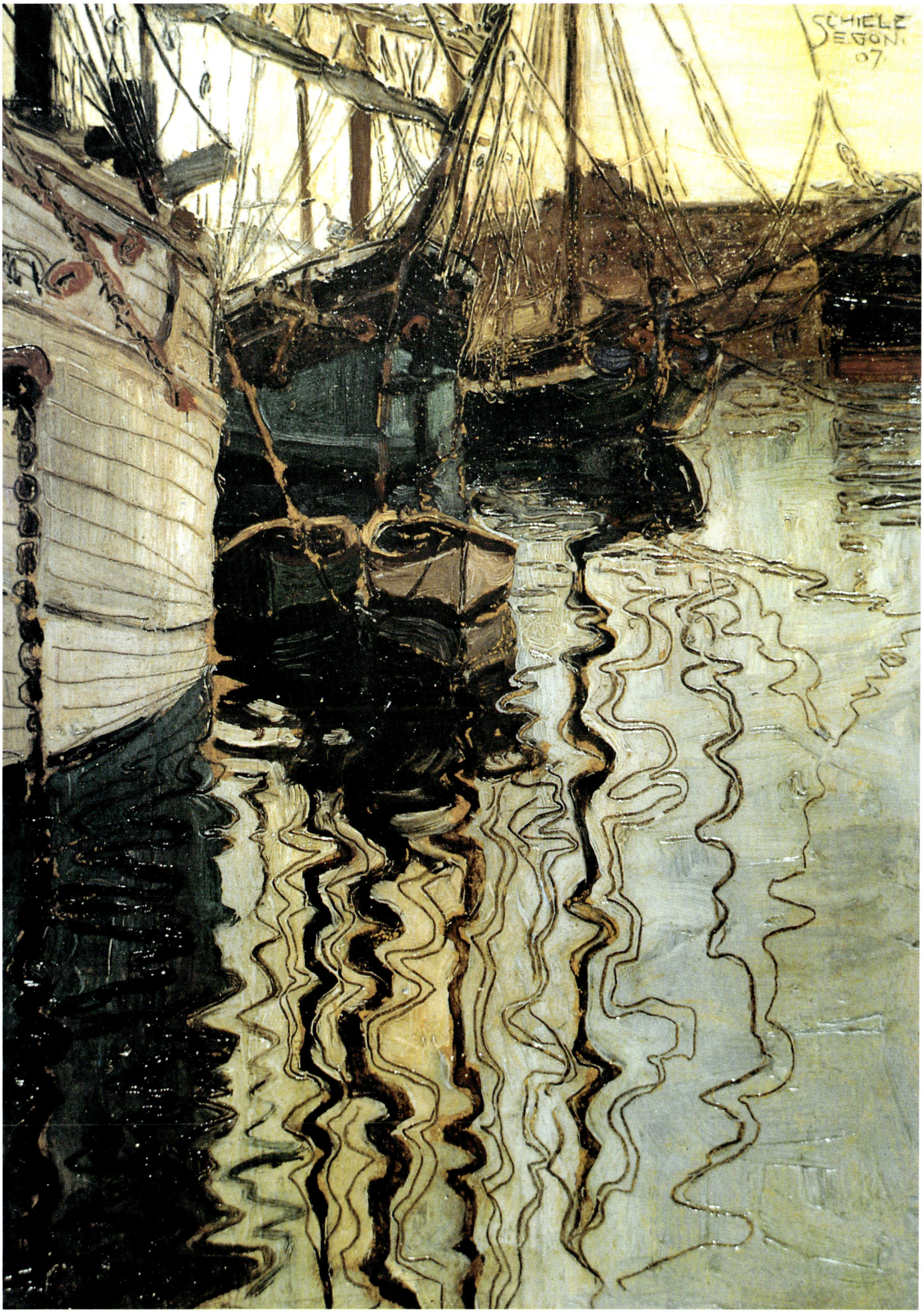
SCHIELE
EGON
07

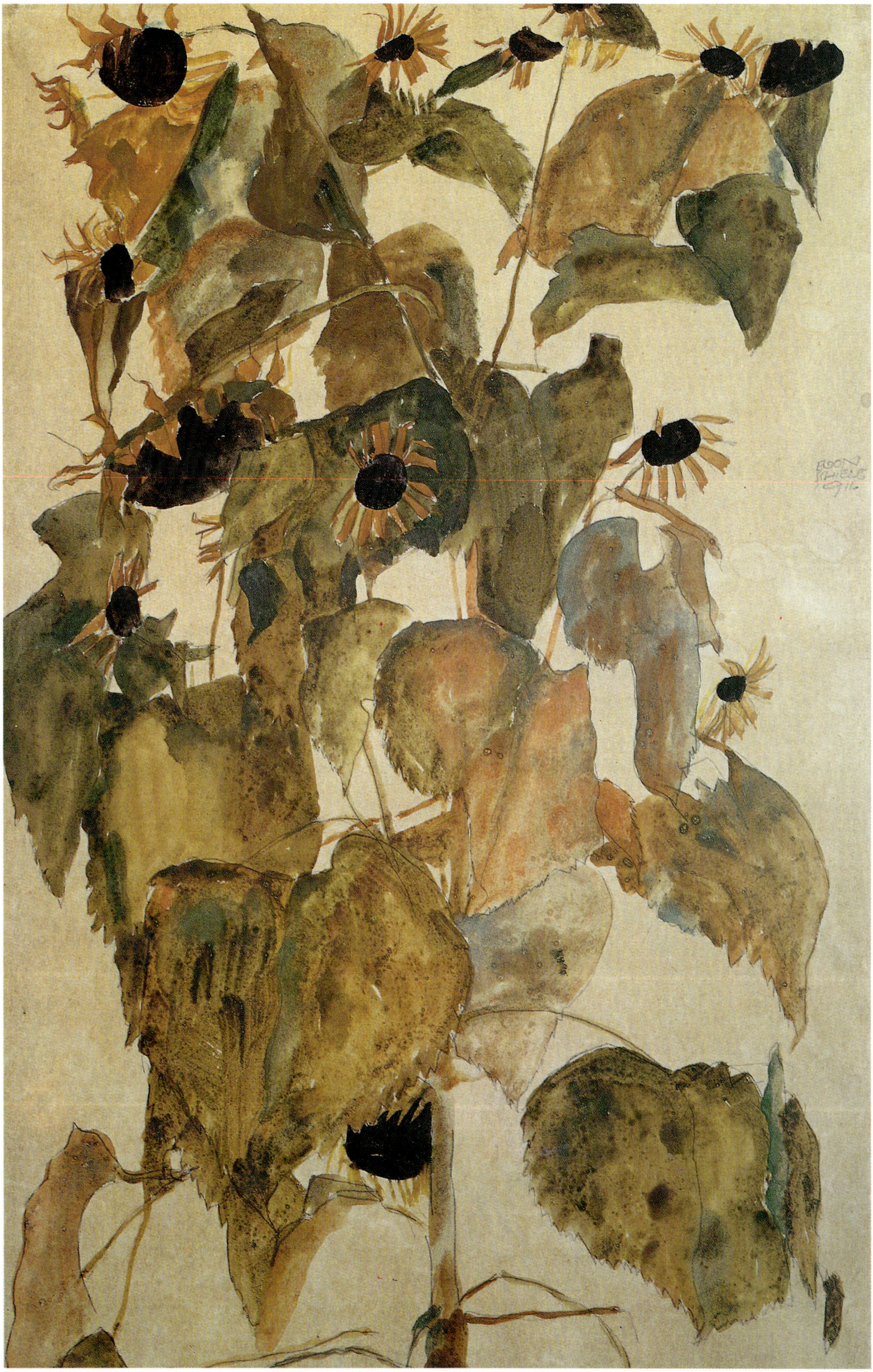
EGON
SCHIELE
1916

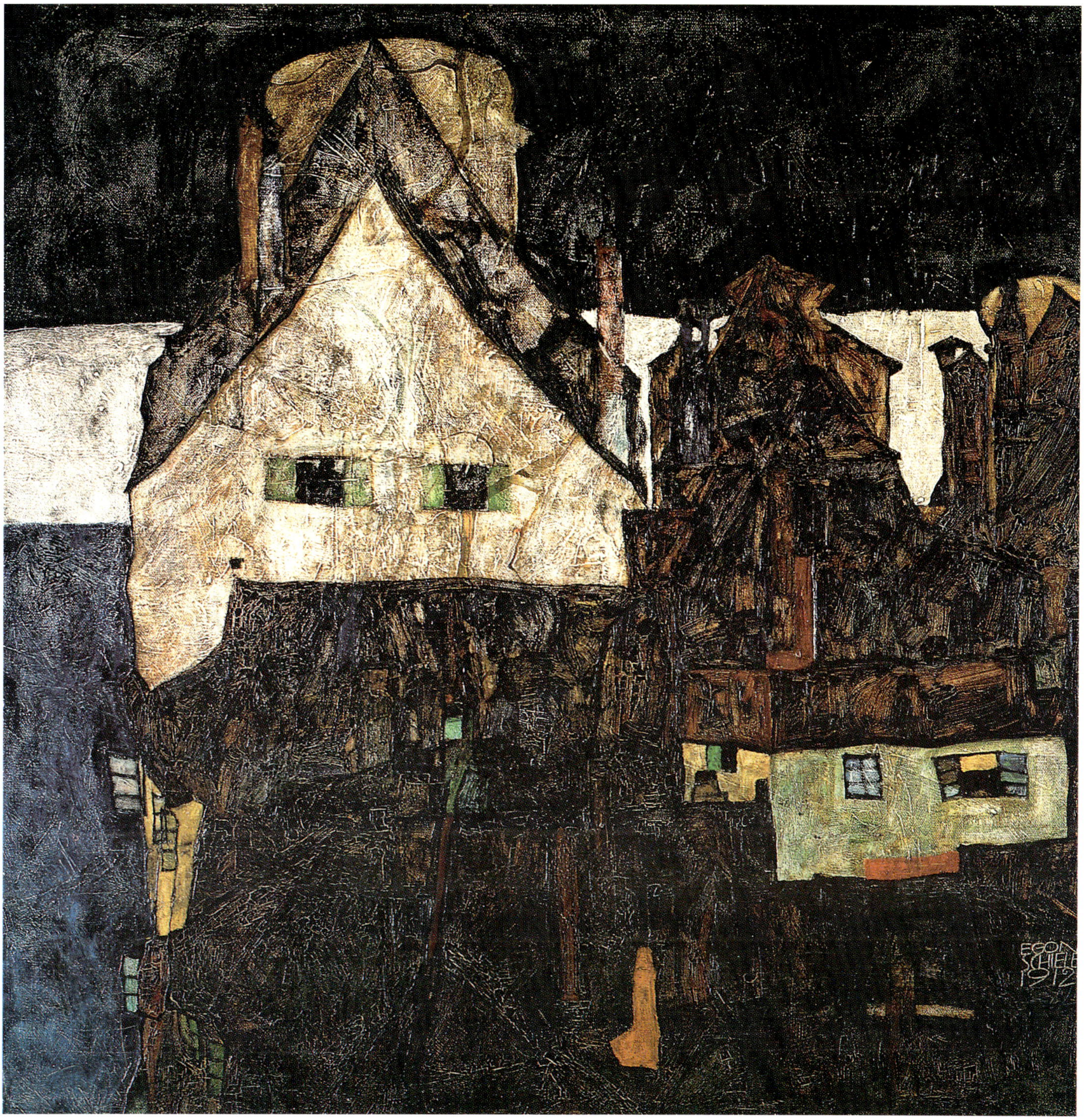

Left:
SUNFLOWER, 1911
Watercolor on paper
Graphische Sammlung Albertina, Vienna

Above:
DEAD CITY, 1912
Oil on canvas, 31½ × 31½ inches (80 × 80 cm)
Kunsthaus, Zurich

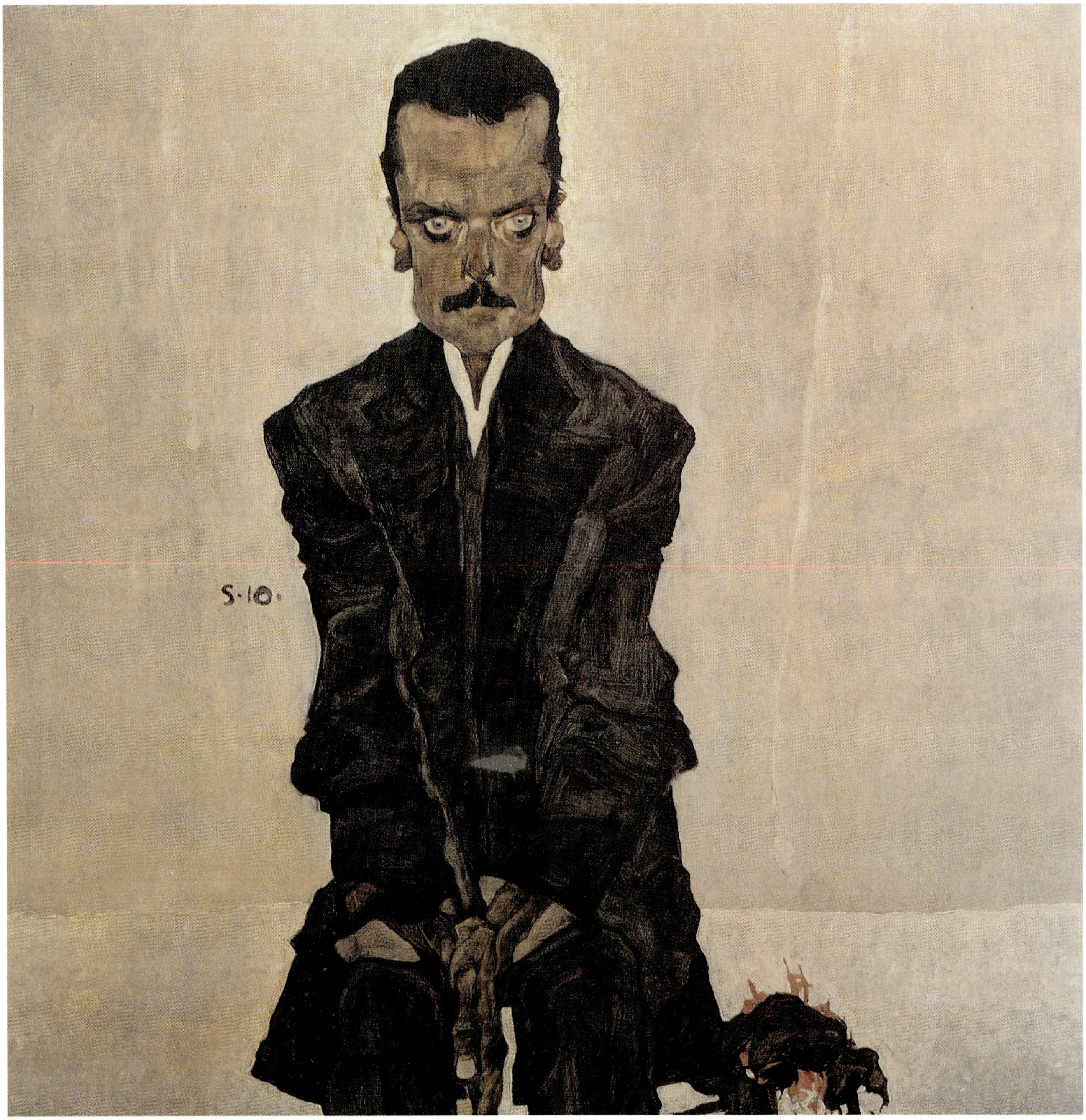

Above:
PORTRAIT OF EDUARD KOSMAK, 1910
Oil on canvas, 39½ × 39½ inches (100 × 100 cm)
Österreichische Galerie, Vienna

Right:
NUDE GIRL WITH CROSSED ARMS (GERTI), 1910
Black chalk and watercolor, 18 × 11 inches (45 × 28 cm)
Graphische Sammlung Albertina, Vienna

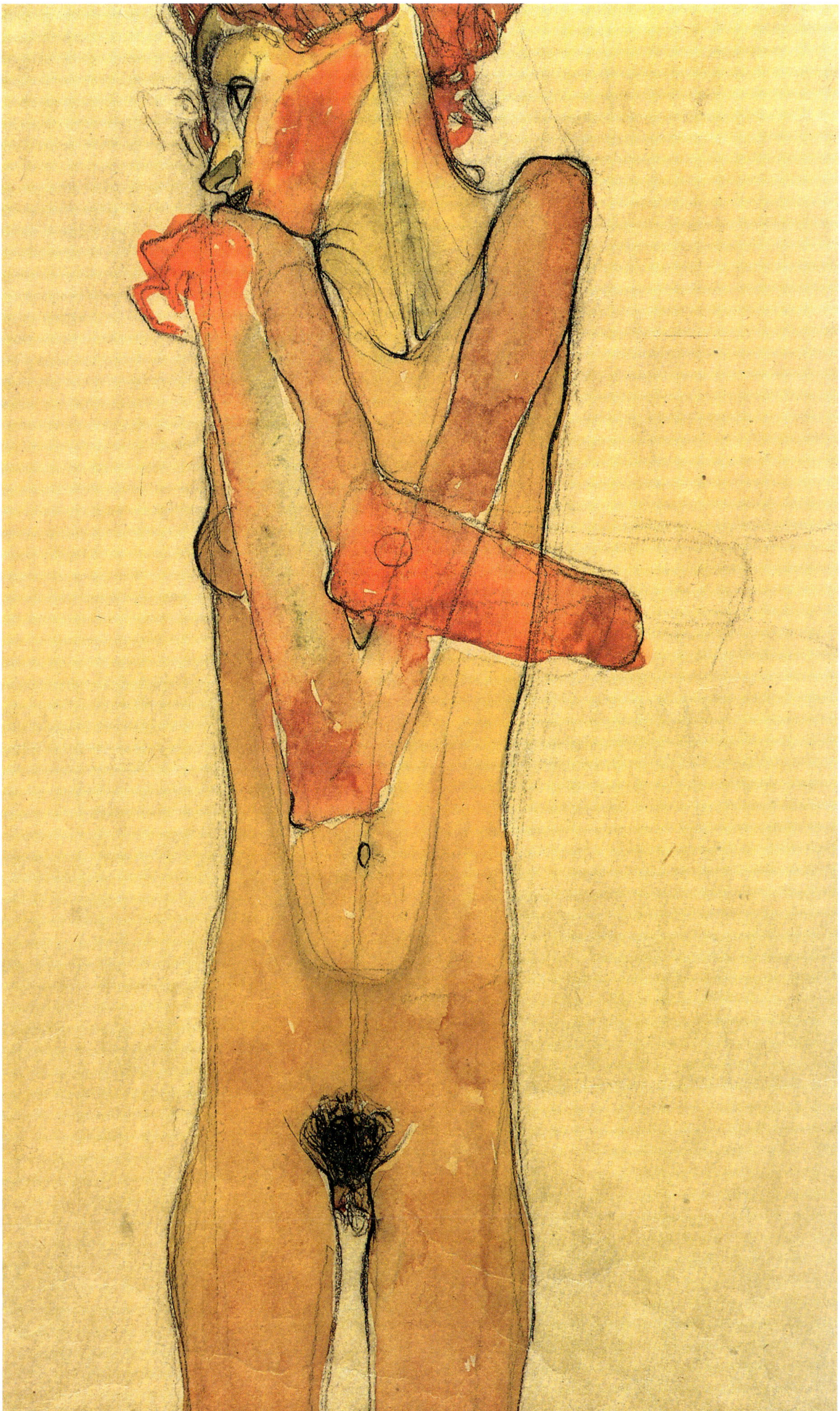

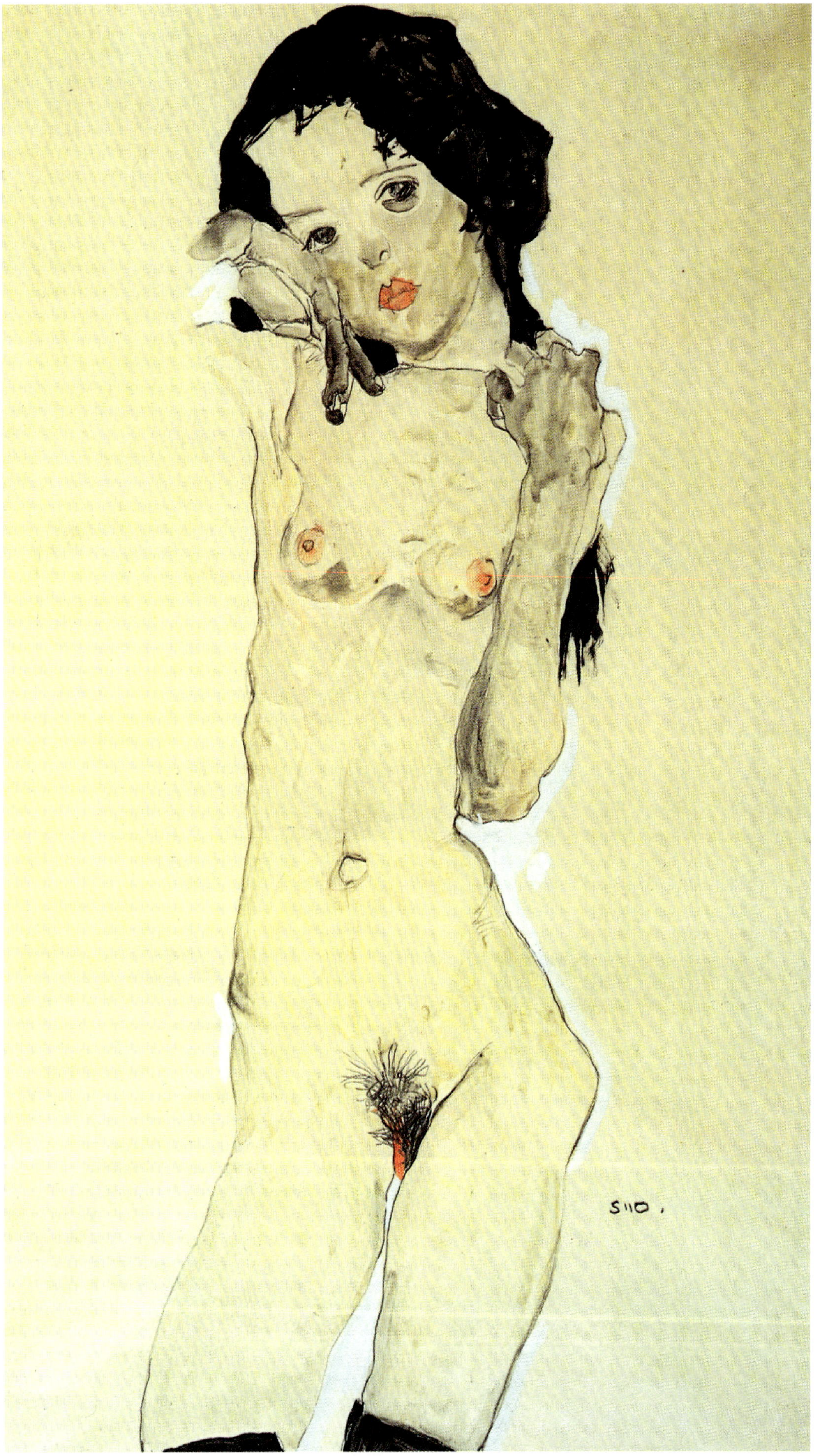

Standing Nude Girl, 1910
Pencil and watercolor, 21¼ × 12 inches (54 × 30 cm)
Graphische Sammlung Albertina, Vienna

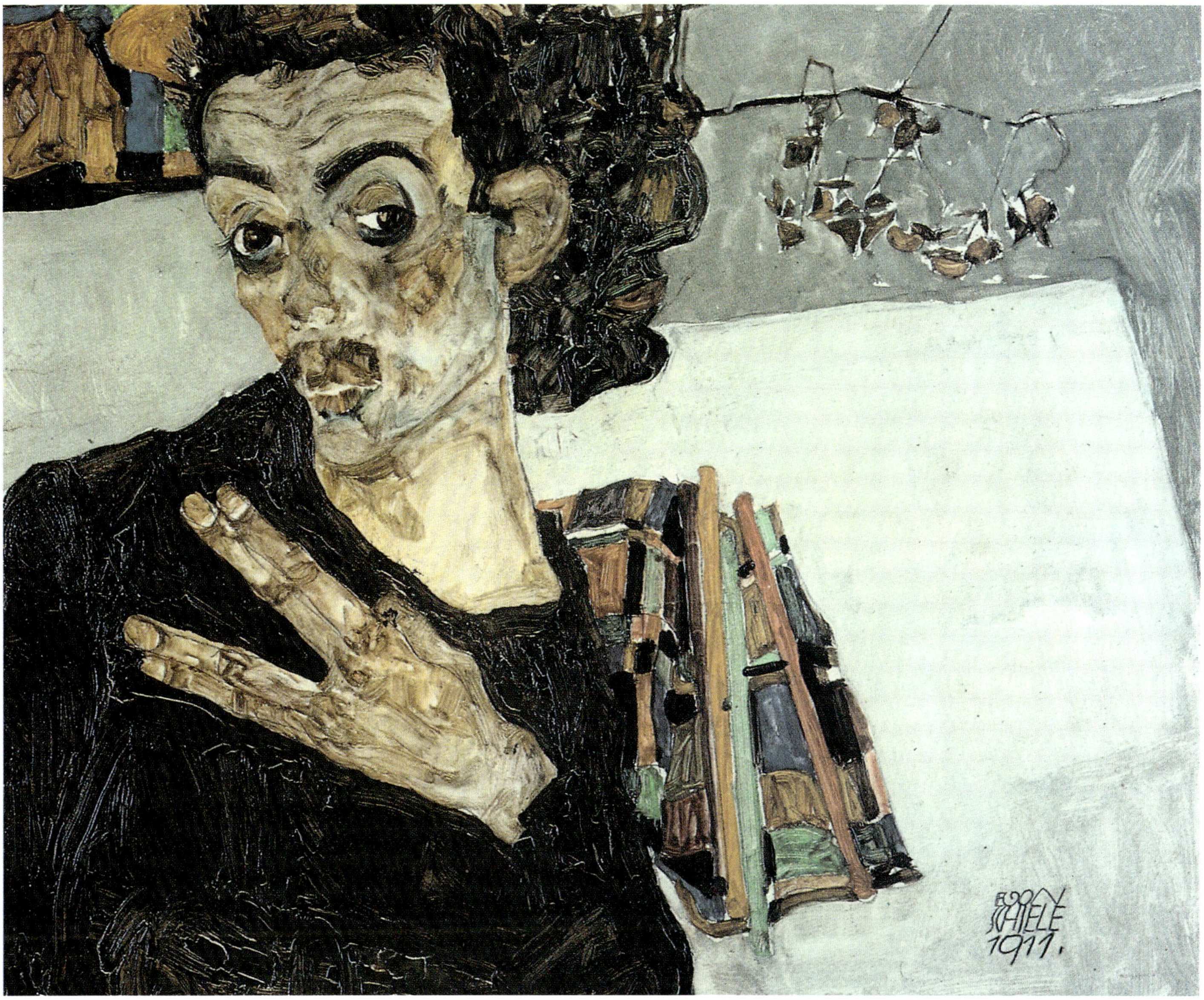

SELF-PORTRAIT WITH BLACK CLAY VASE, 1911
Oil on wooden panel, 10⅞ × 13⅜ inches (27.5 × 34 cm)
Historisches Museum der Stadt Wien, Vienna

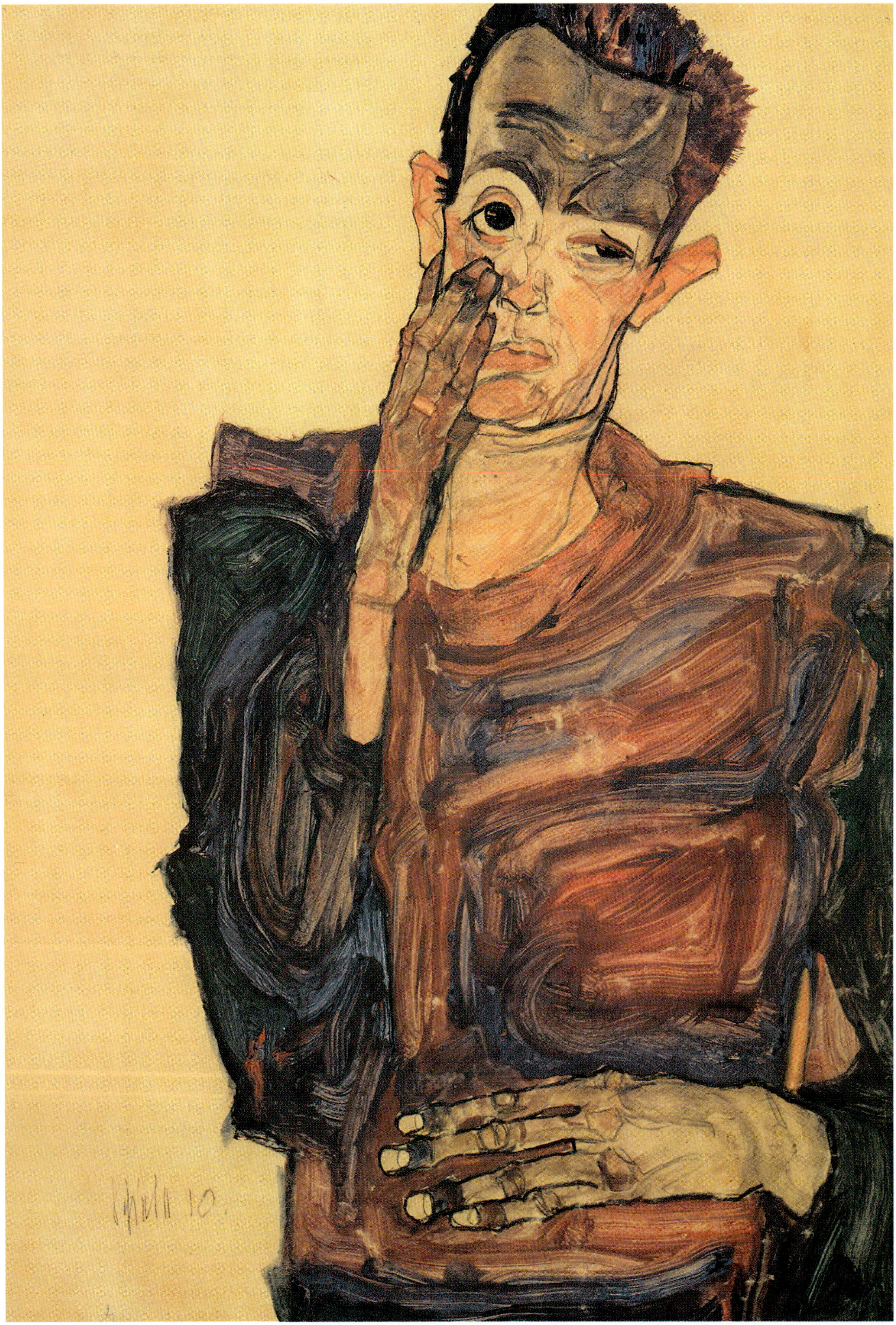

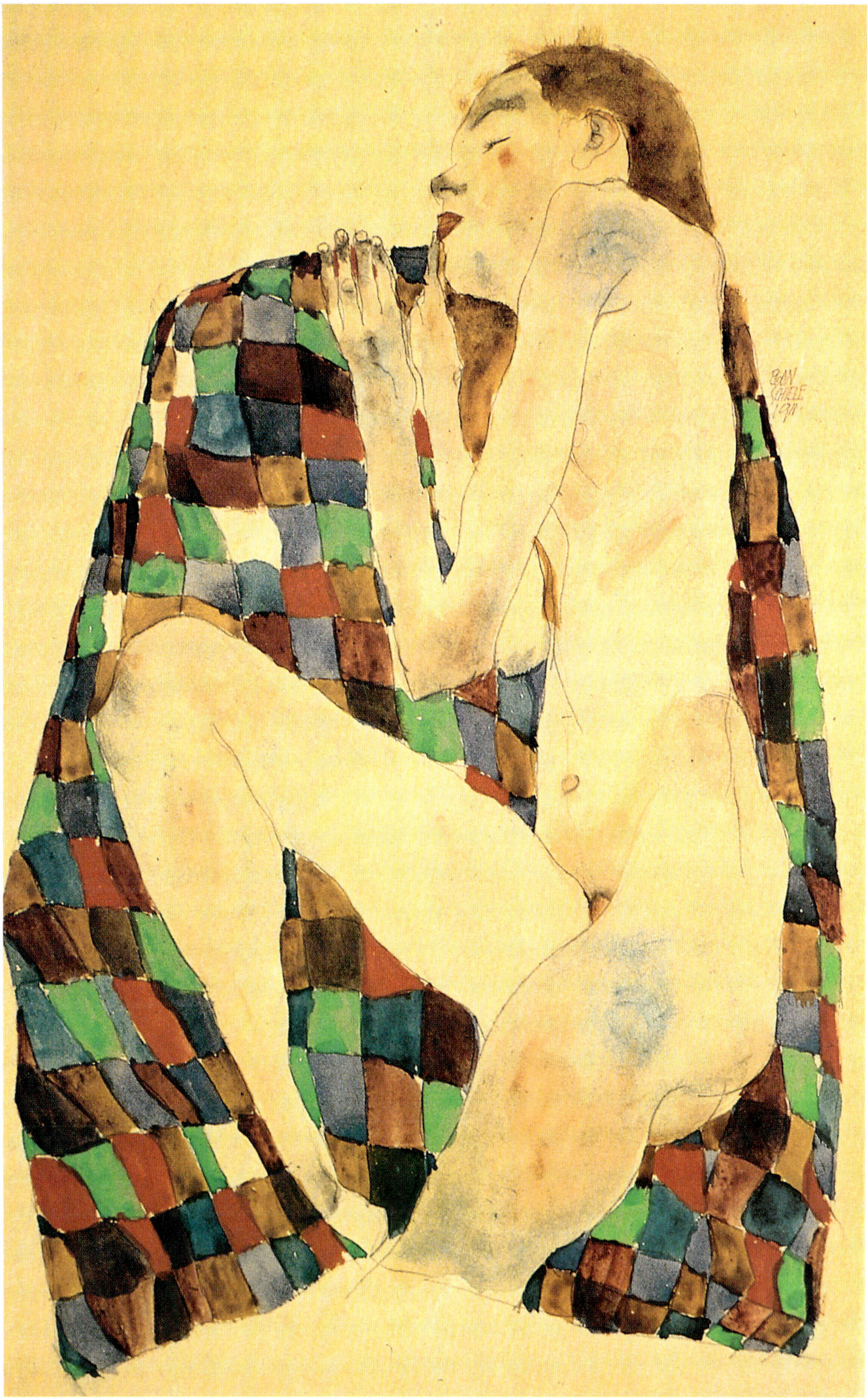

Left:
Self-Portrait Pulling Cheek, 1910
Black chalk, watercolor, and gouache, 17½ × 12 inches
(44.5 × 30.5 cm)
Graphische Sammlung Albertina, Vienna

Above:
Nude Against a Colored Background , 1911
Pencil, watercolor, and gouache, 19 × 12½ inches
(49 × 31 cm)
Neue Galerie der Stadt, Graz

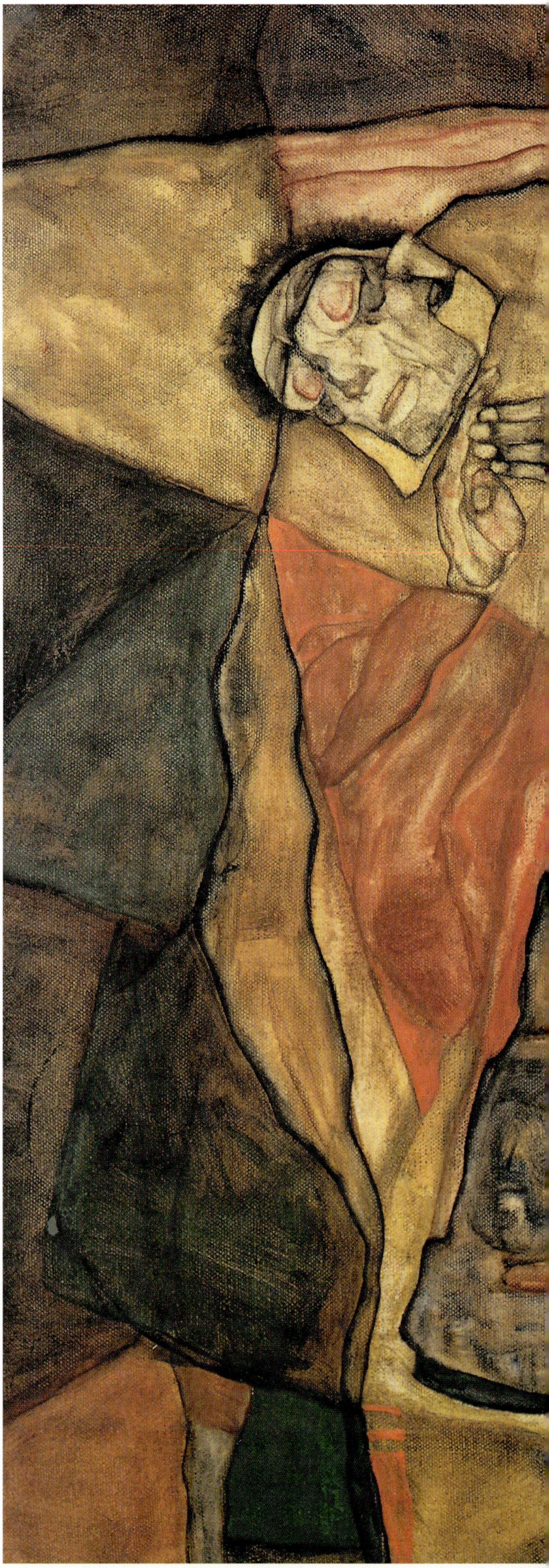

Agony, 1912
Oil on canvas, 27½ × 31½ inches (70 × 80 cm)
Neue Pinakothek, Munich

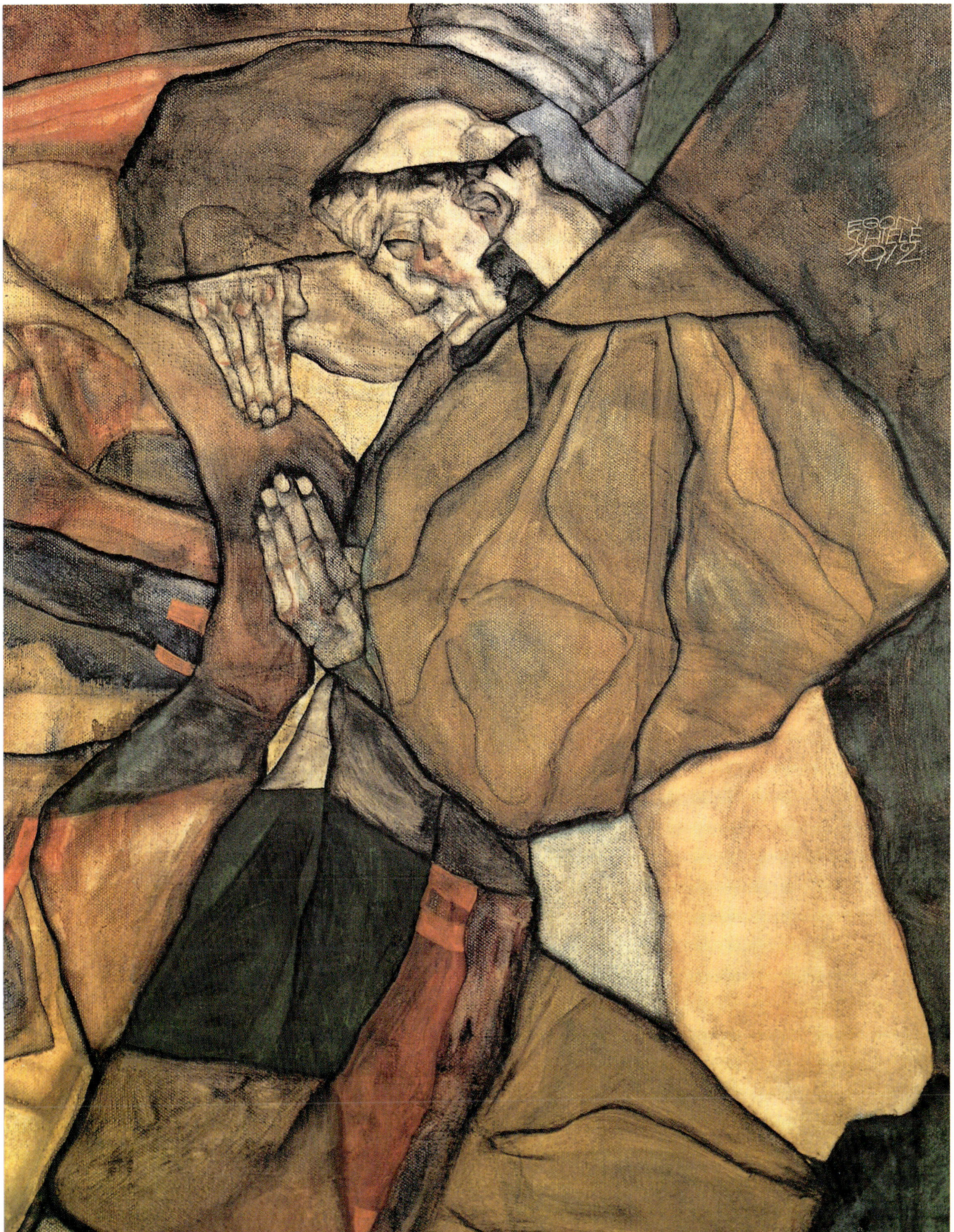
EGON
SCHIELE
1912

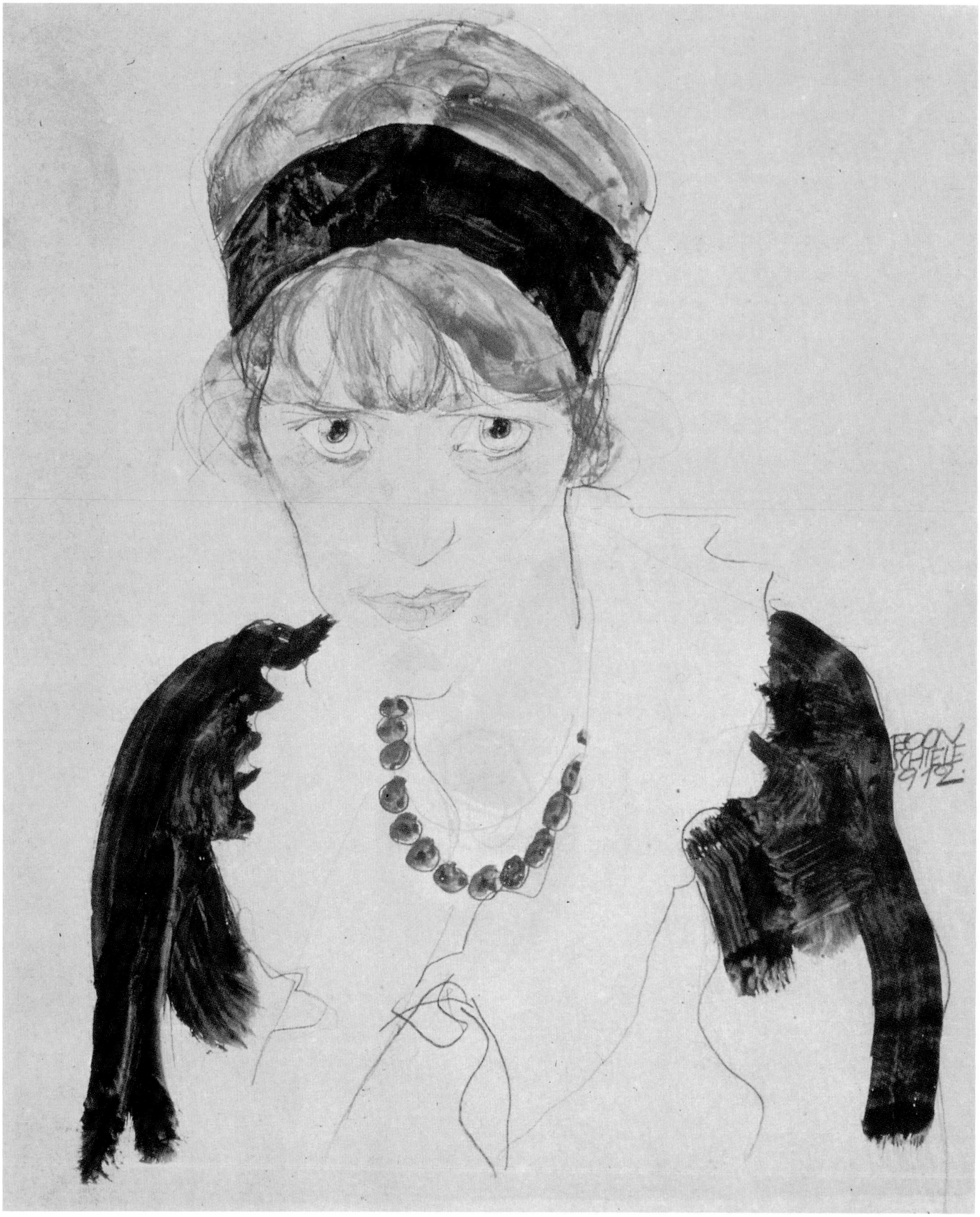

Above:
WALLY, 1912
Pencil and gouache, 11½ × 10½ inches (29.2 × 26.7 cm)
Private Collection
Photograph Galerie Im Griechenbeisl, Vienna

Right:
PORTRAIT OF ERICH LEDERER, 1912-13
Oil on canvas, 39½ × 11 inches (101 × 28 cm)
Öffentliche Kunstsammlung, Kunstmuseum, Basel

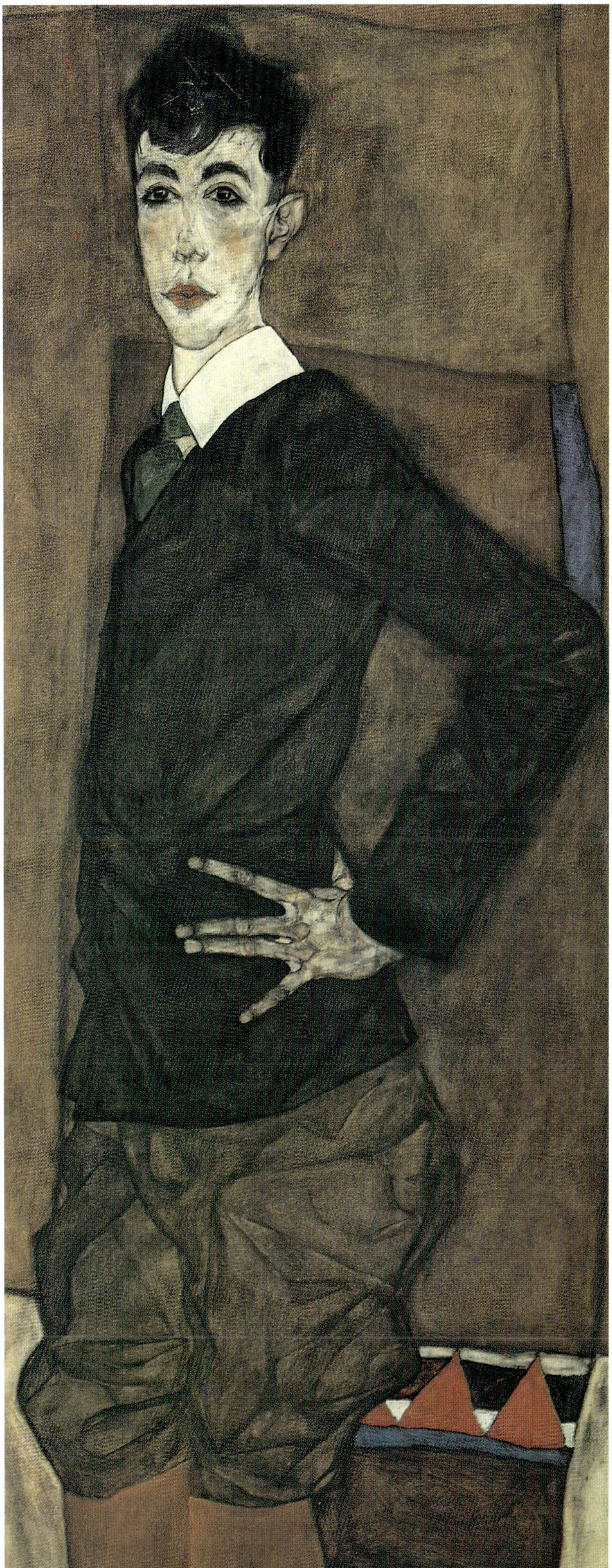

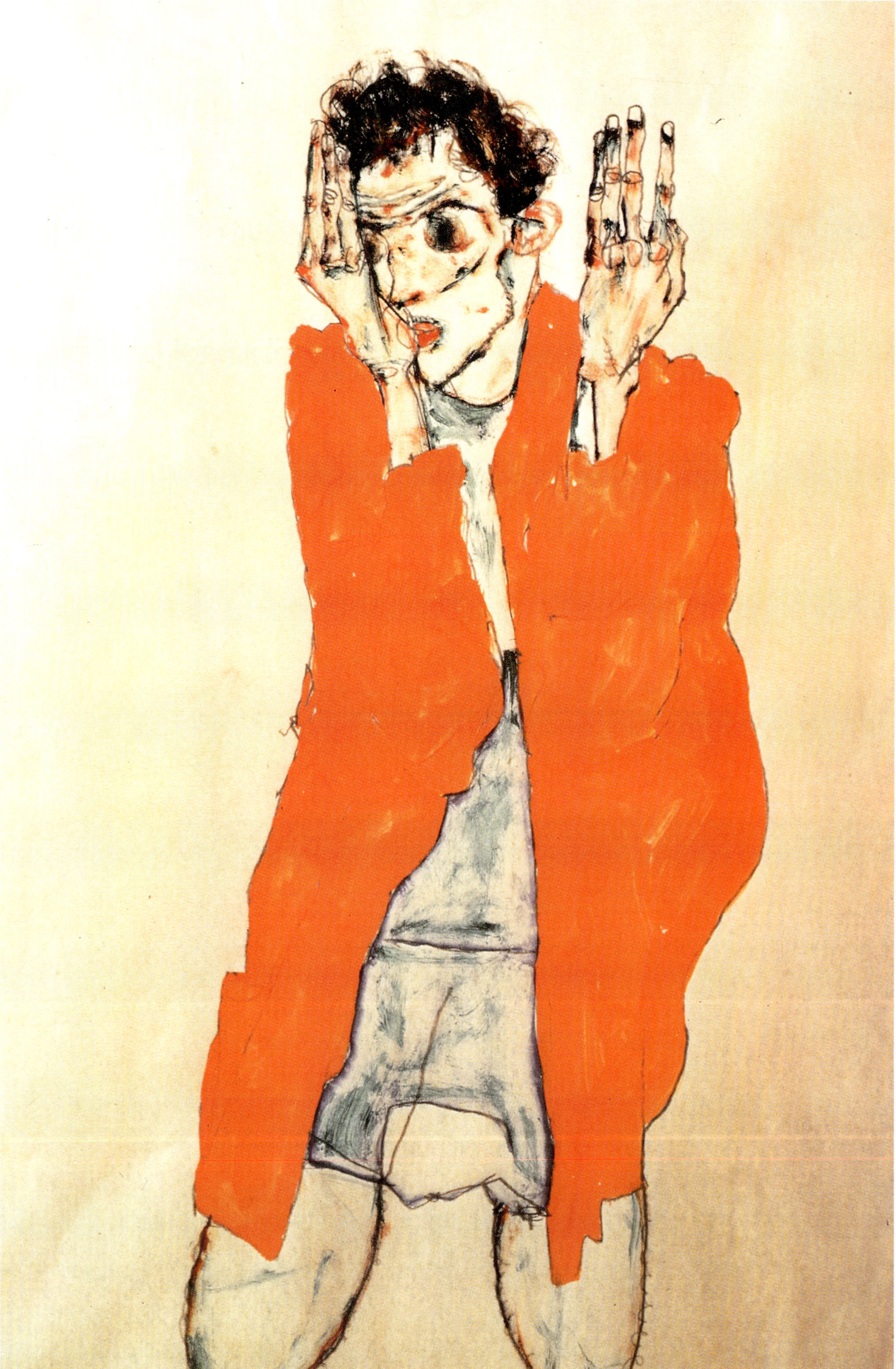

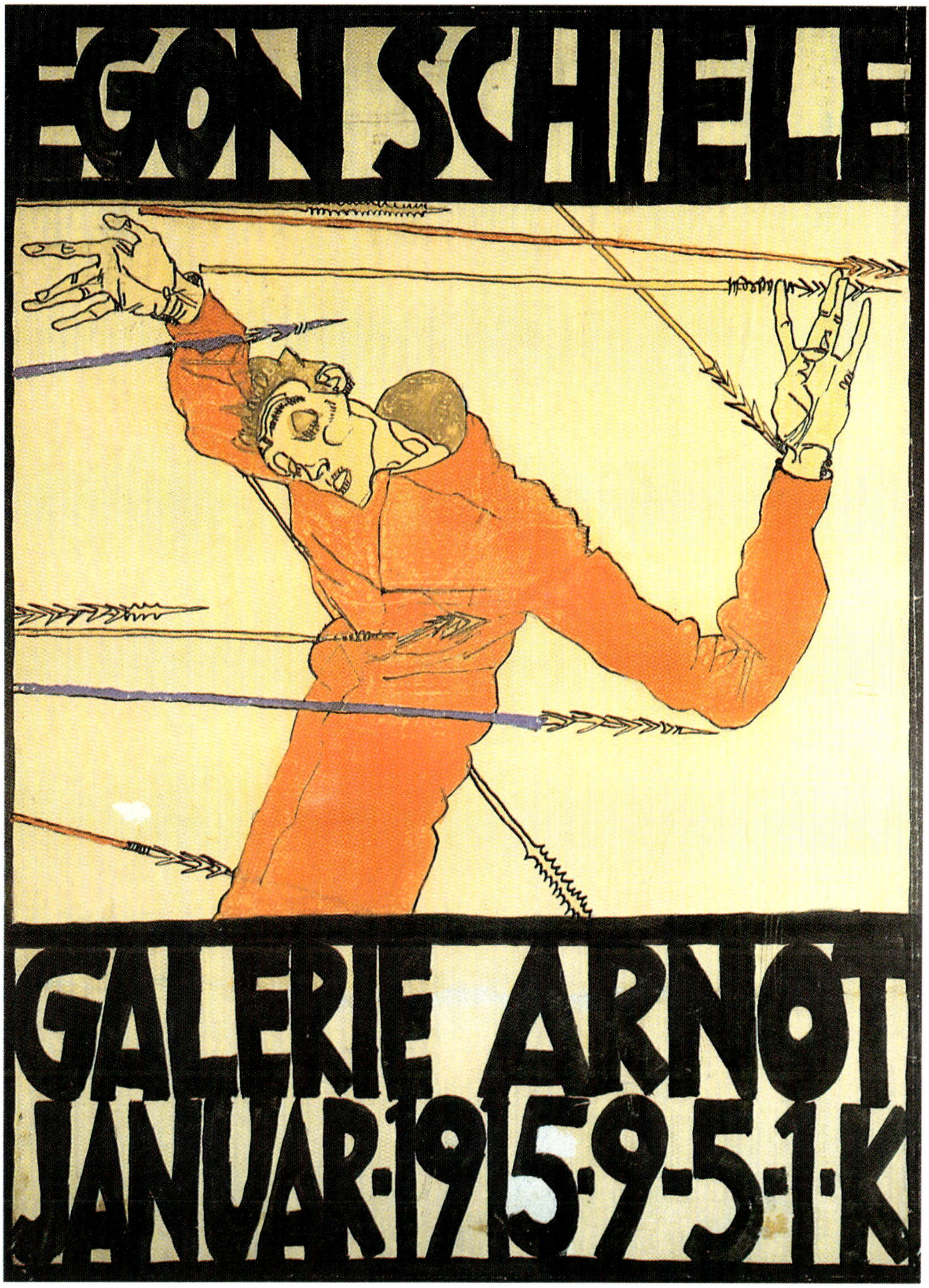

Left:
Self-Portrait with Raised Arms, 1913-14
Black chalk and gouache, 19¼ × 12½ inches
(49 × 31.5 cm)
Private Collection

Above:
Self-Portrait as Saint Sebastian, 1914-15
Indian ink and gouache, 26⅓ × 19¹¹⁄₁₆ inches (67 × 50 cm)
Historisches Museum der Stadt Wien, Vienna

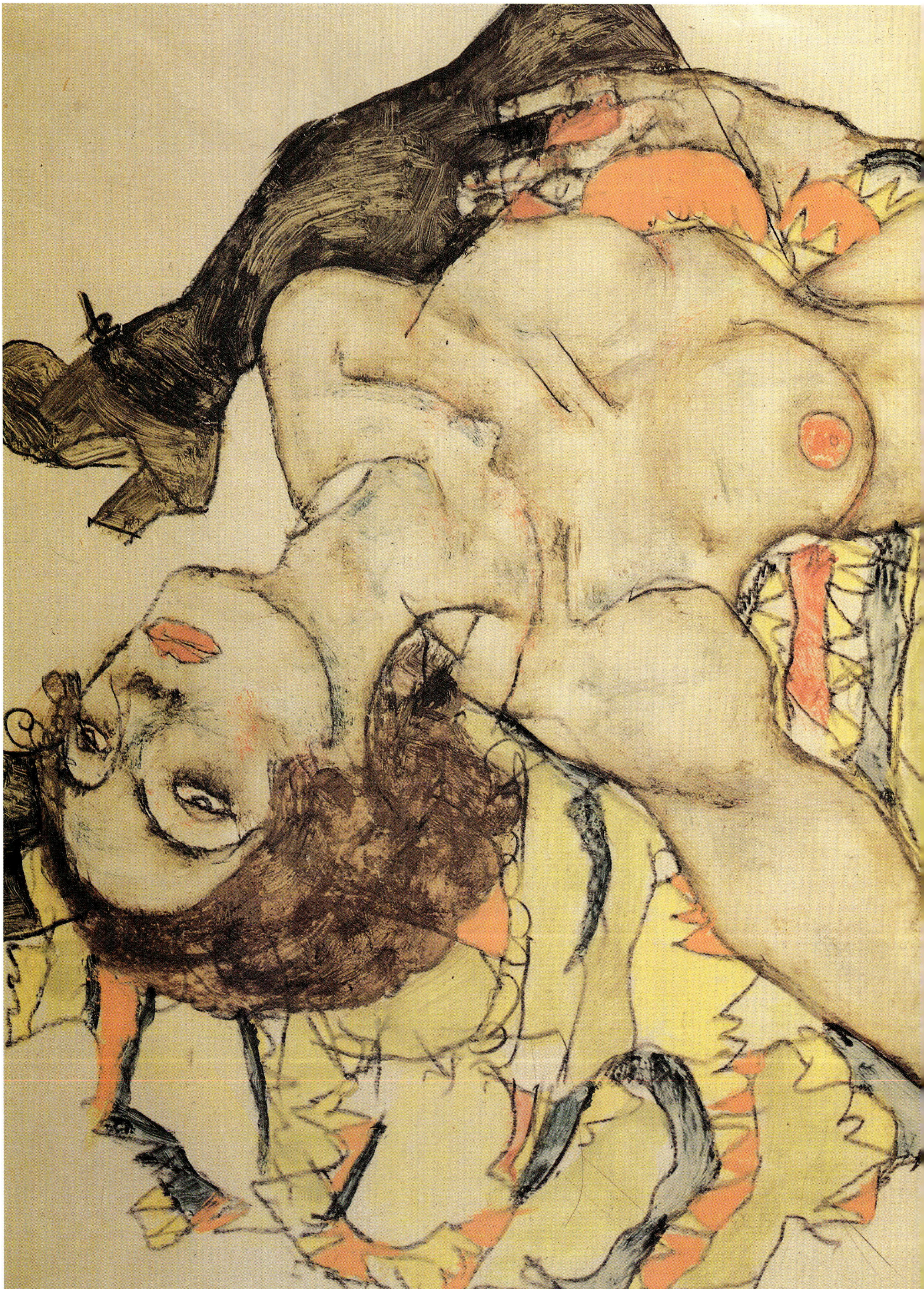

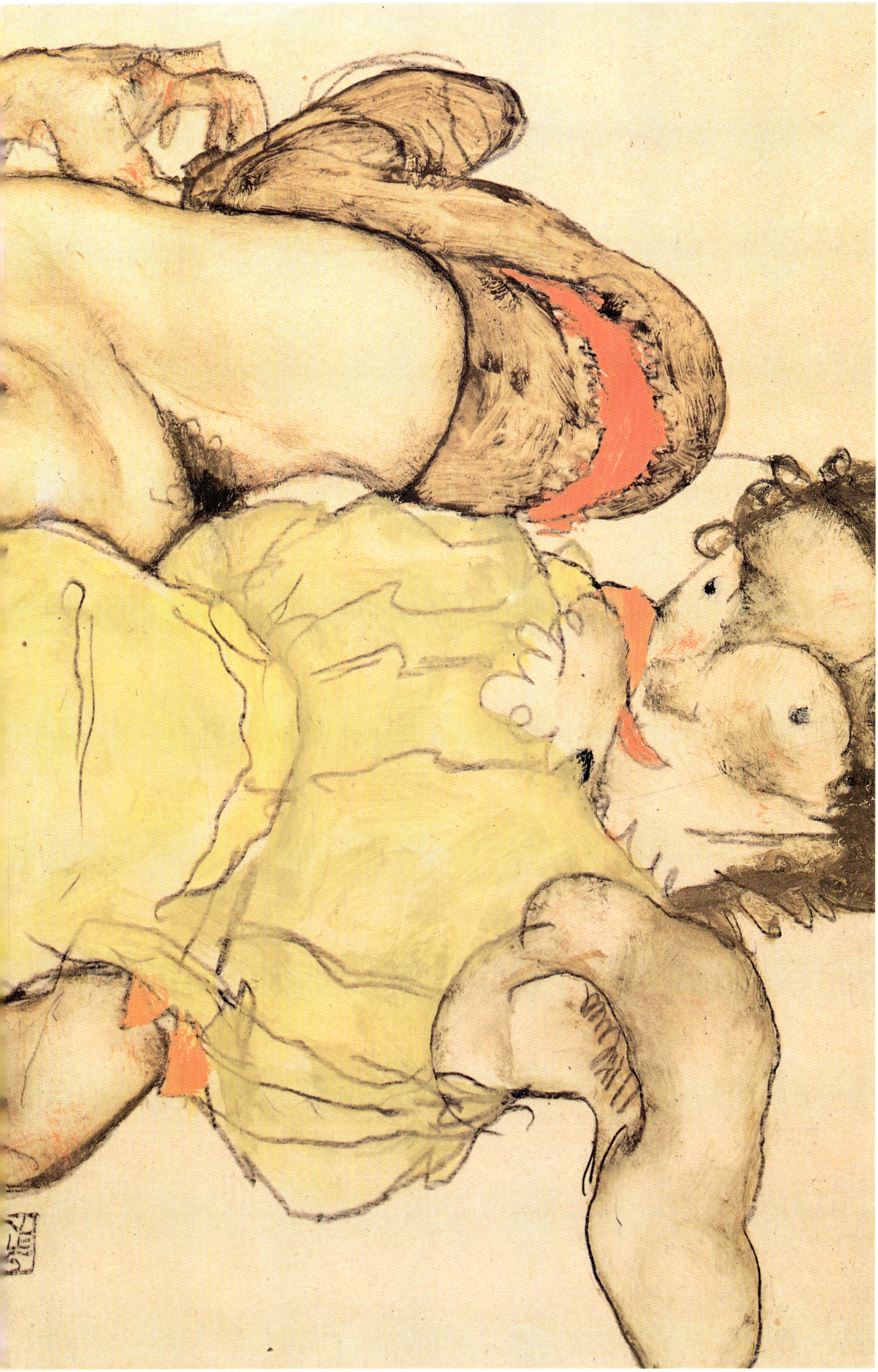

Previous pages:
TWO GIRLS LYING ENTWINED, 1915
Pencil, watercolor, and gouache, 13 × 20 inches (32.5 × 50 cm)
Graphische Sammlung Albertina, Vienna

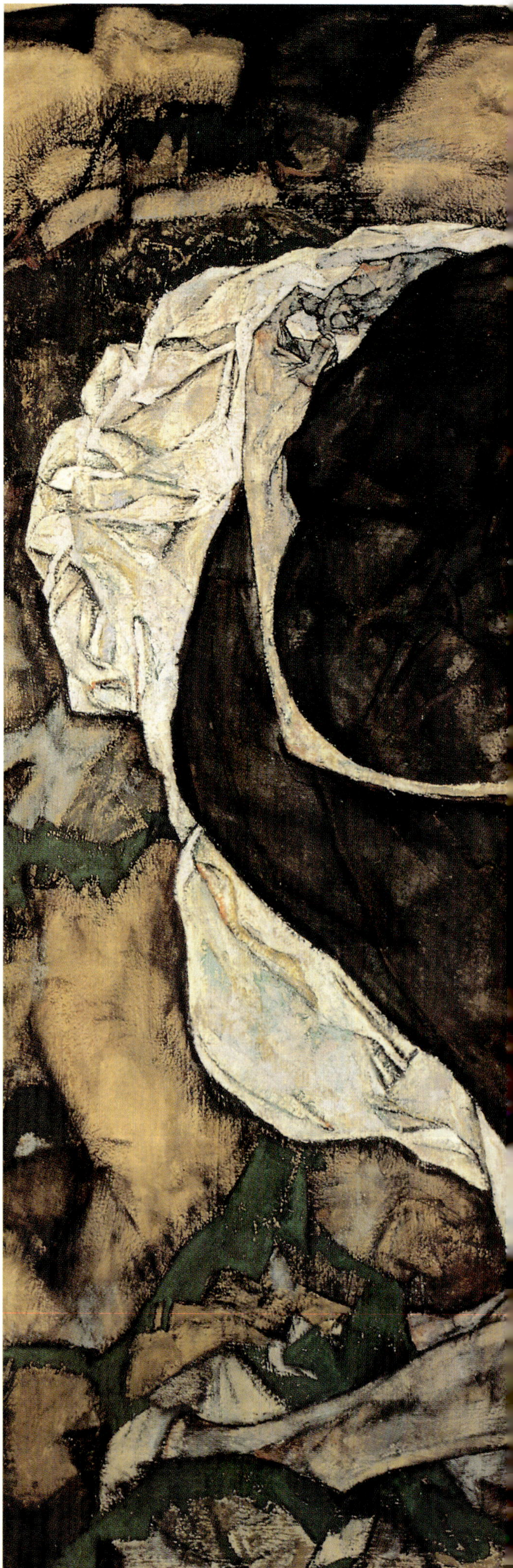

Right:
DEATH AND THE MAIDEN, 1915
Oil on canvas, 59 × 70⅞ inches (150 × 180 cm)
Österreichische Galerie, Vienna

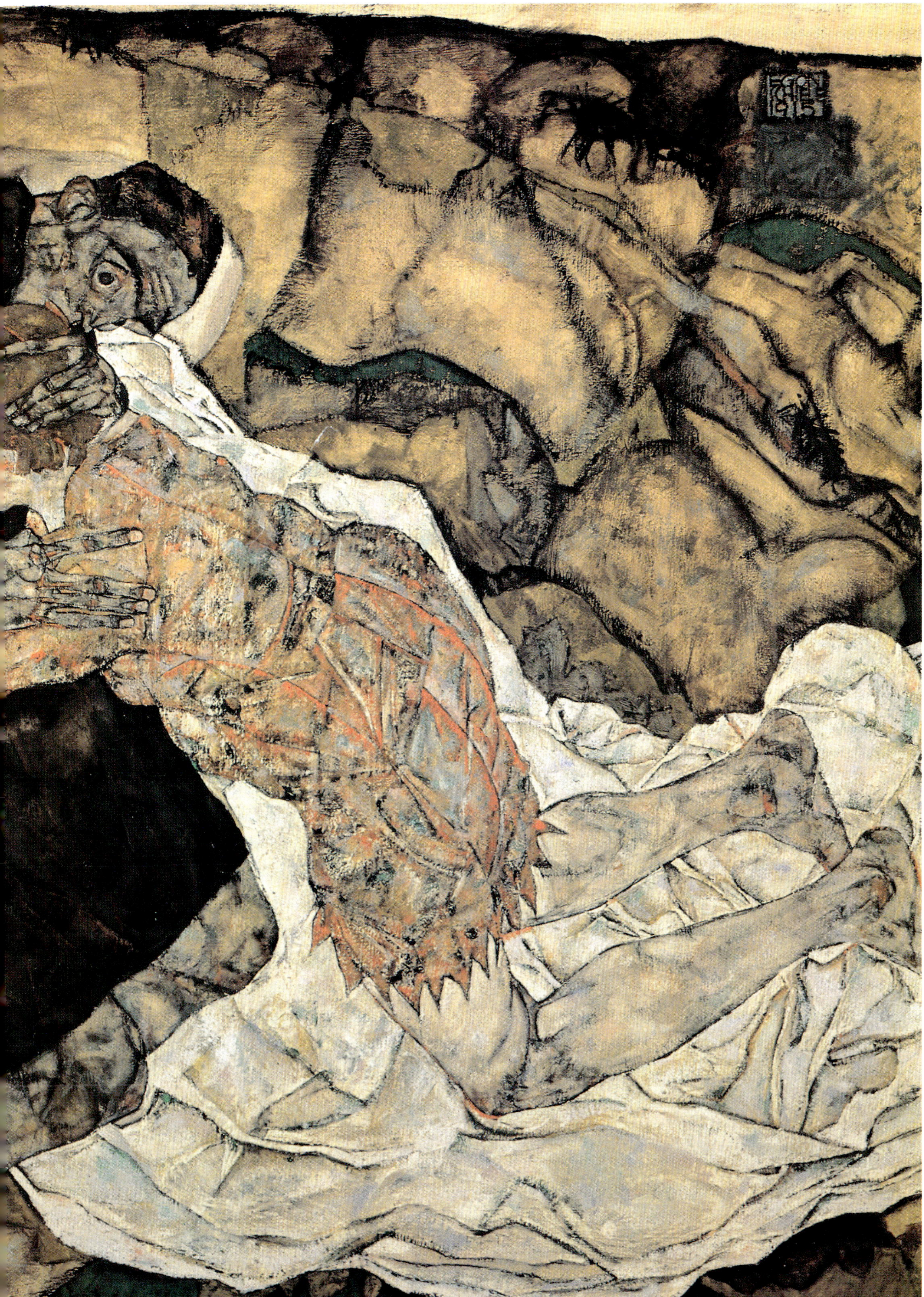

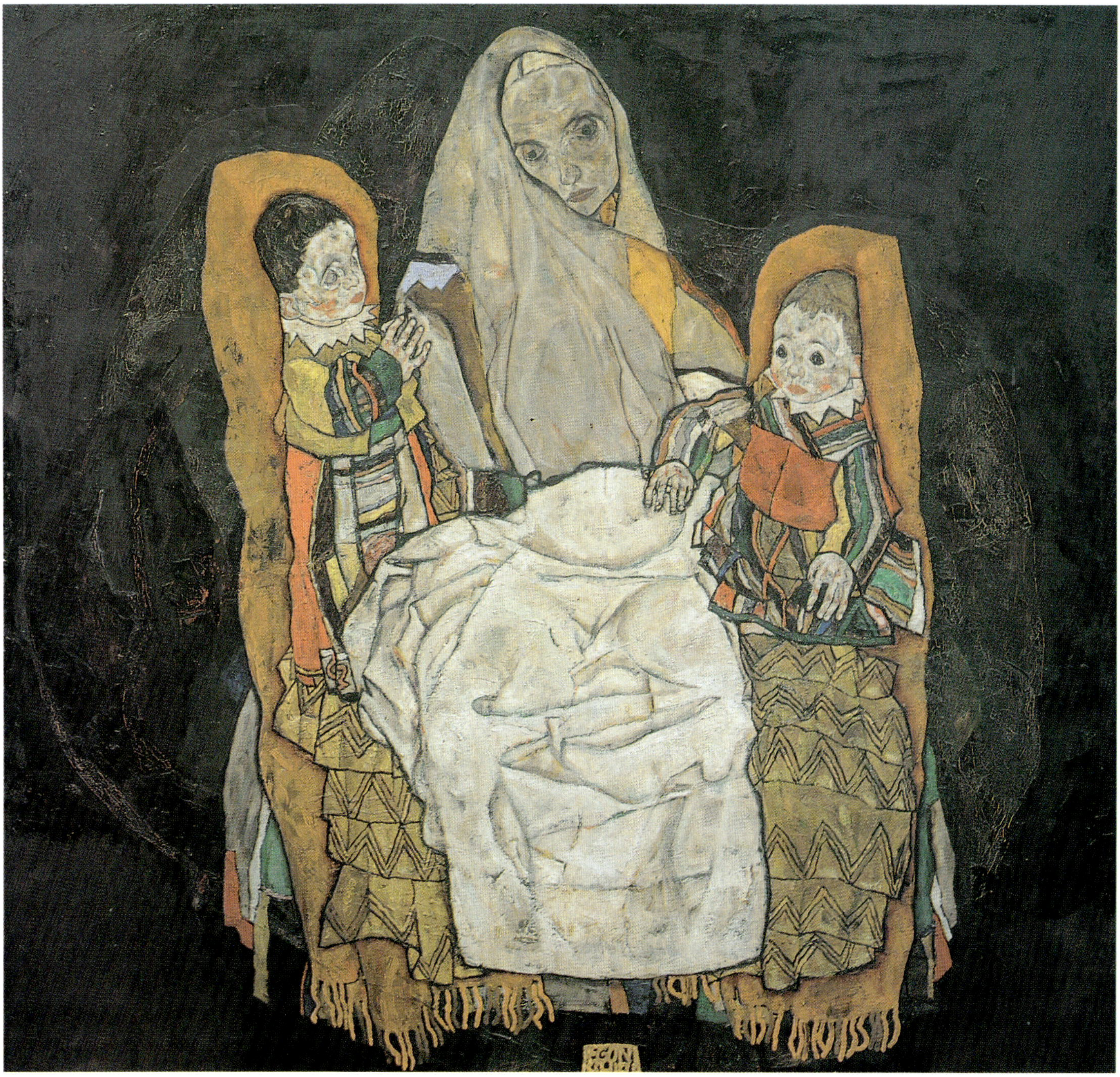

Above:
Mother with Two Children, 1915
Oil on canvas, 59 × 62½ inches (150 × 159 cm)
Österreichische Galerie, Vienna

Right:
Portrait of Edith, Standing, 1915
Oil on canvas, 71 × 43 inches (180 × 110 cm)
Haags Gemeentemuseum, The Hague

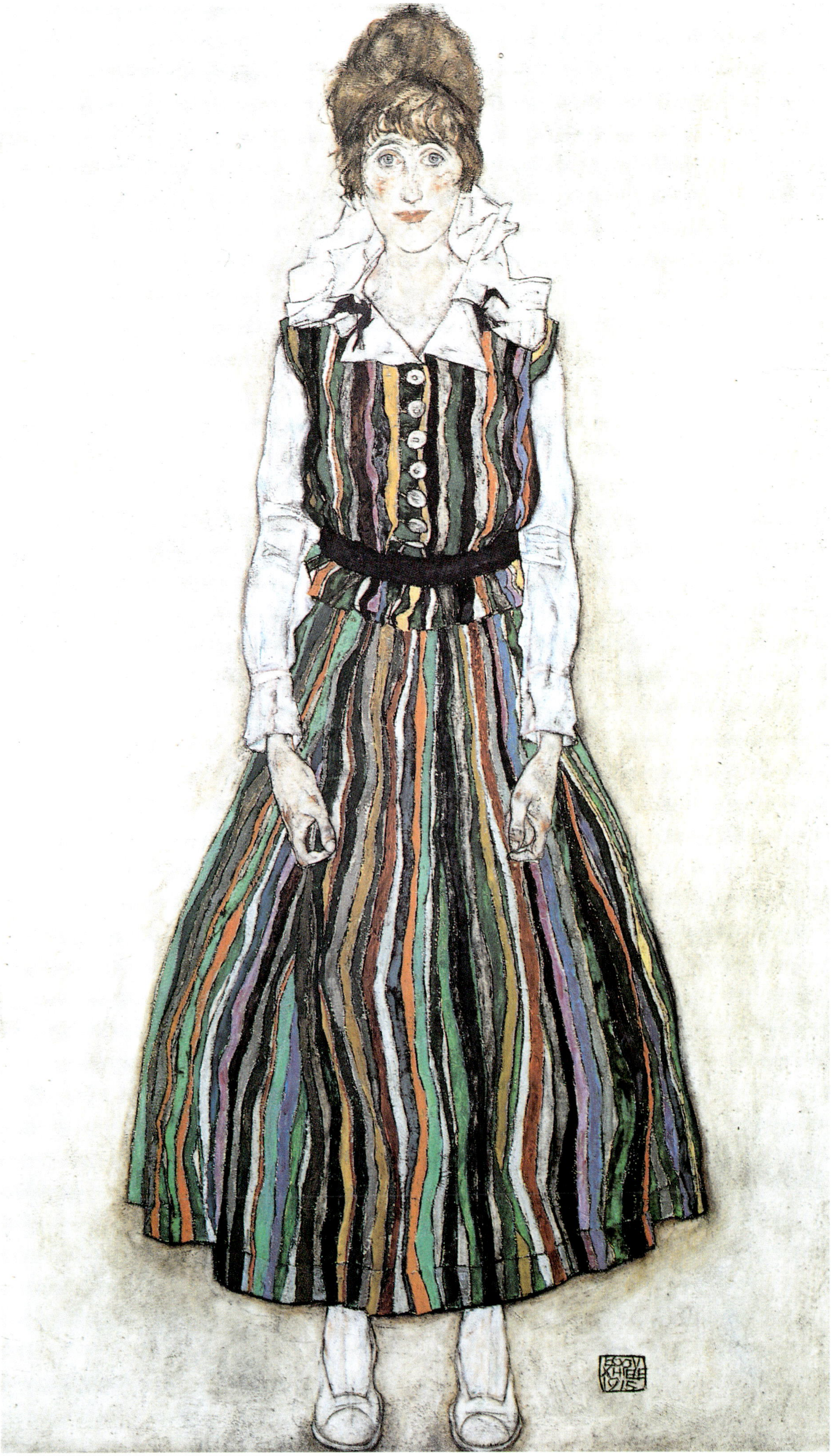
EGON
SCHIELE
1915

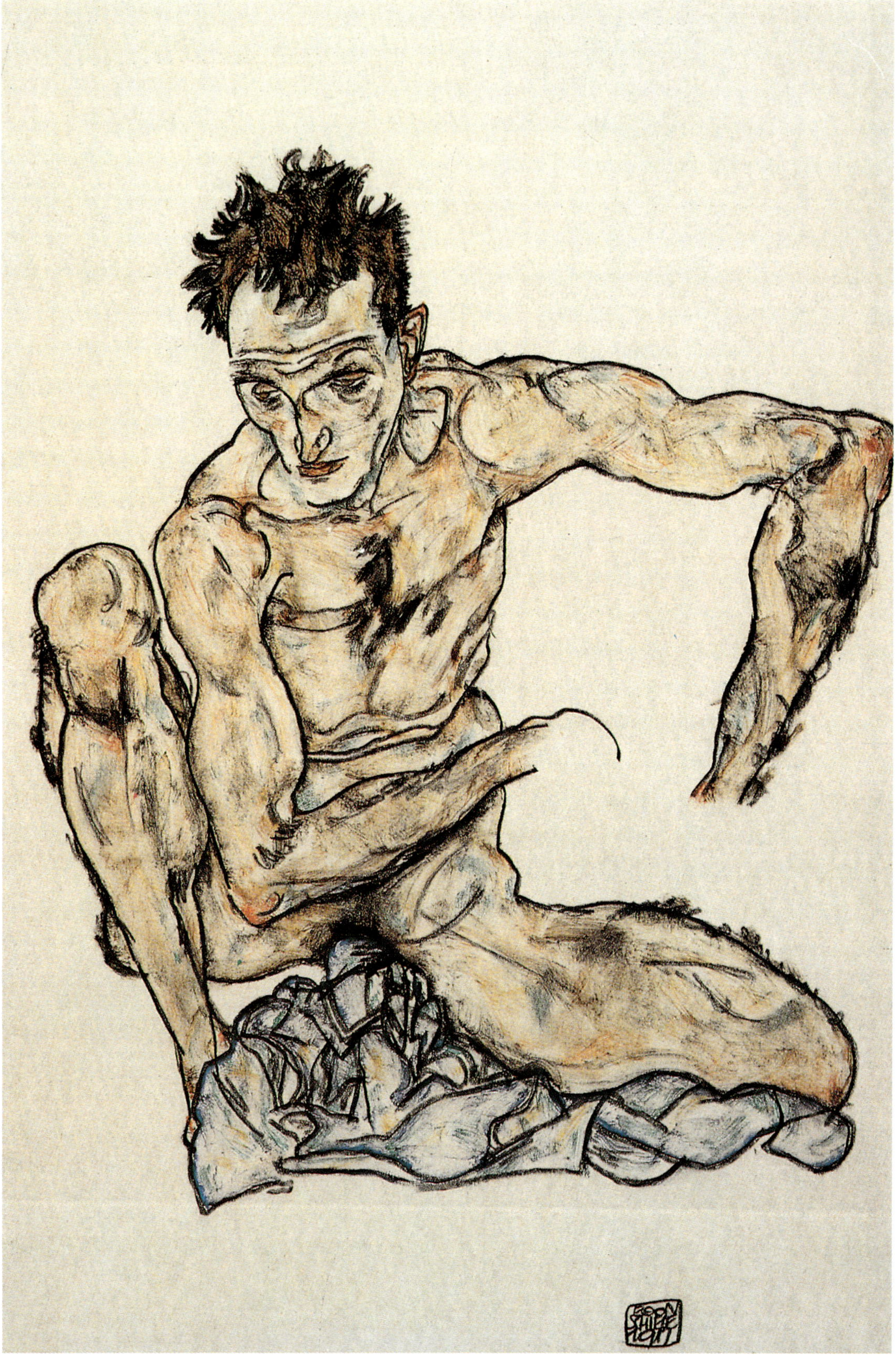

Self-Portrait Squatting, 1916
Chalk and watercolor
Graphische Sammlung Albertina, Vienna

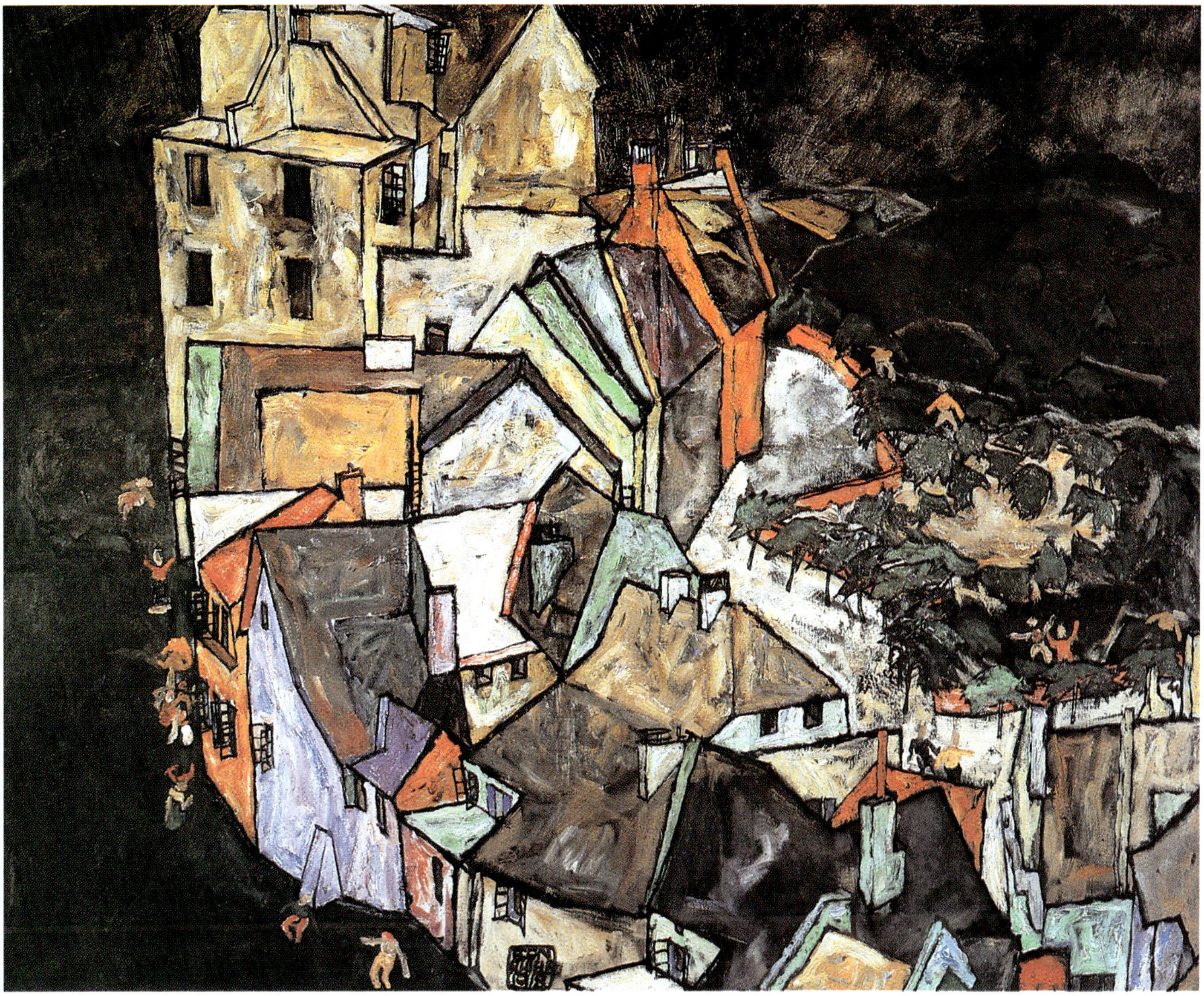

EDGE OF TOWN, 1917
Oil on canvas, 43¹⁄₁₀ × 54⁹⁄₁₀ inches (109.5 × 139.5 cm)
Neue Galerie am Landesmuseum Joanneum, Graz

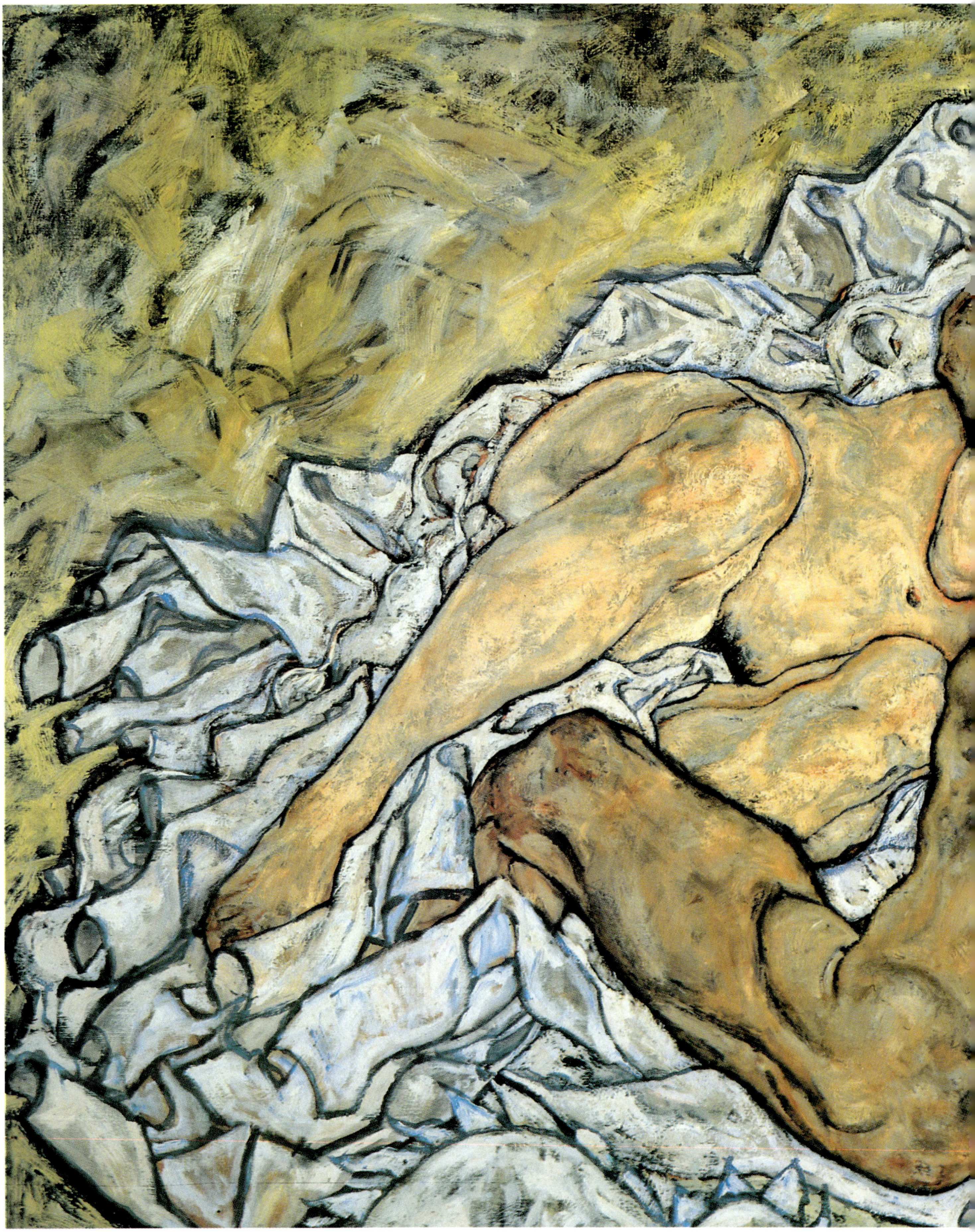

The Embrace, 1917
Oil on canvas, 47 × 67 inches (119.4 × 170.2 cm)
Österreichische Galerie, Vienna

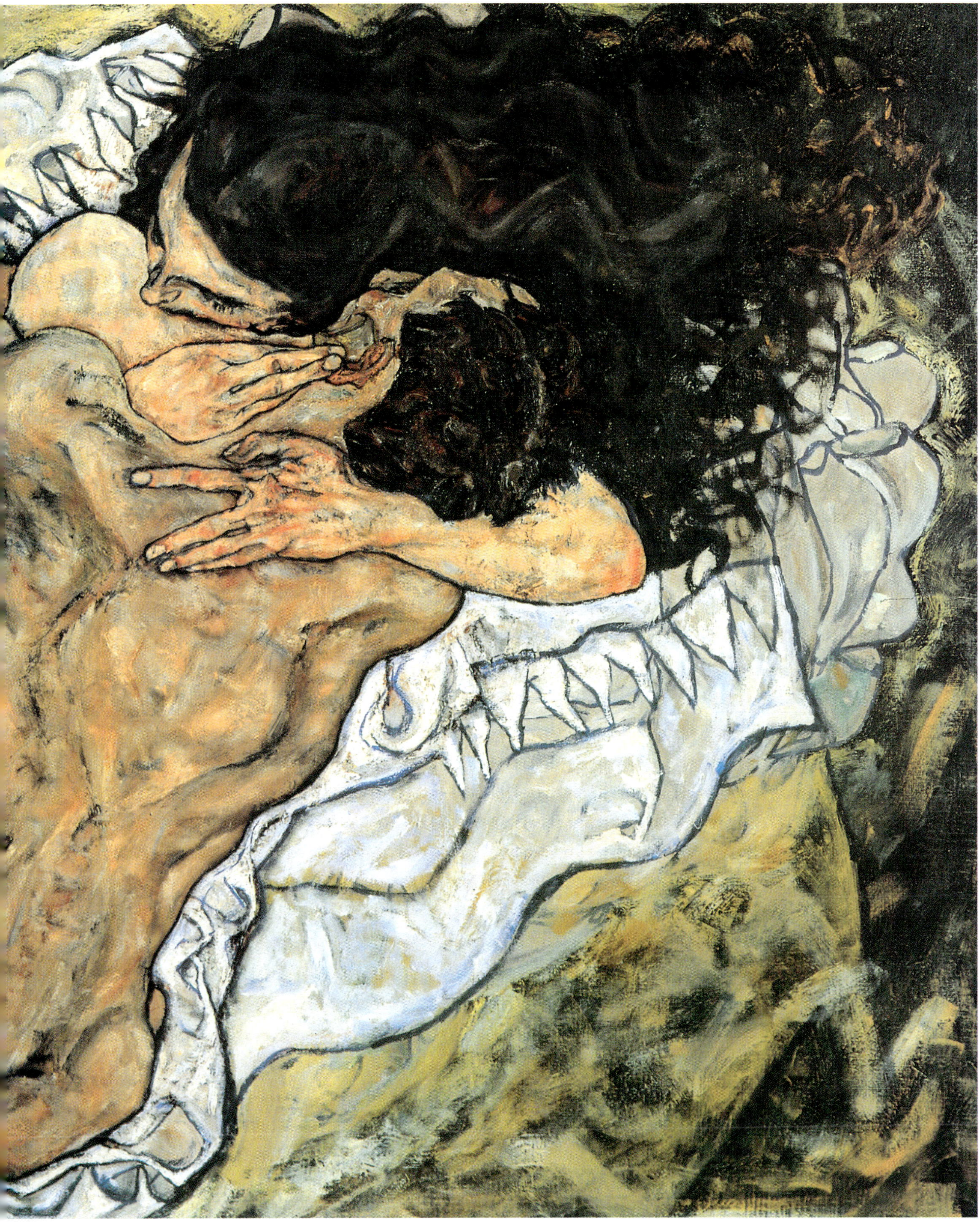

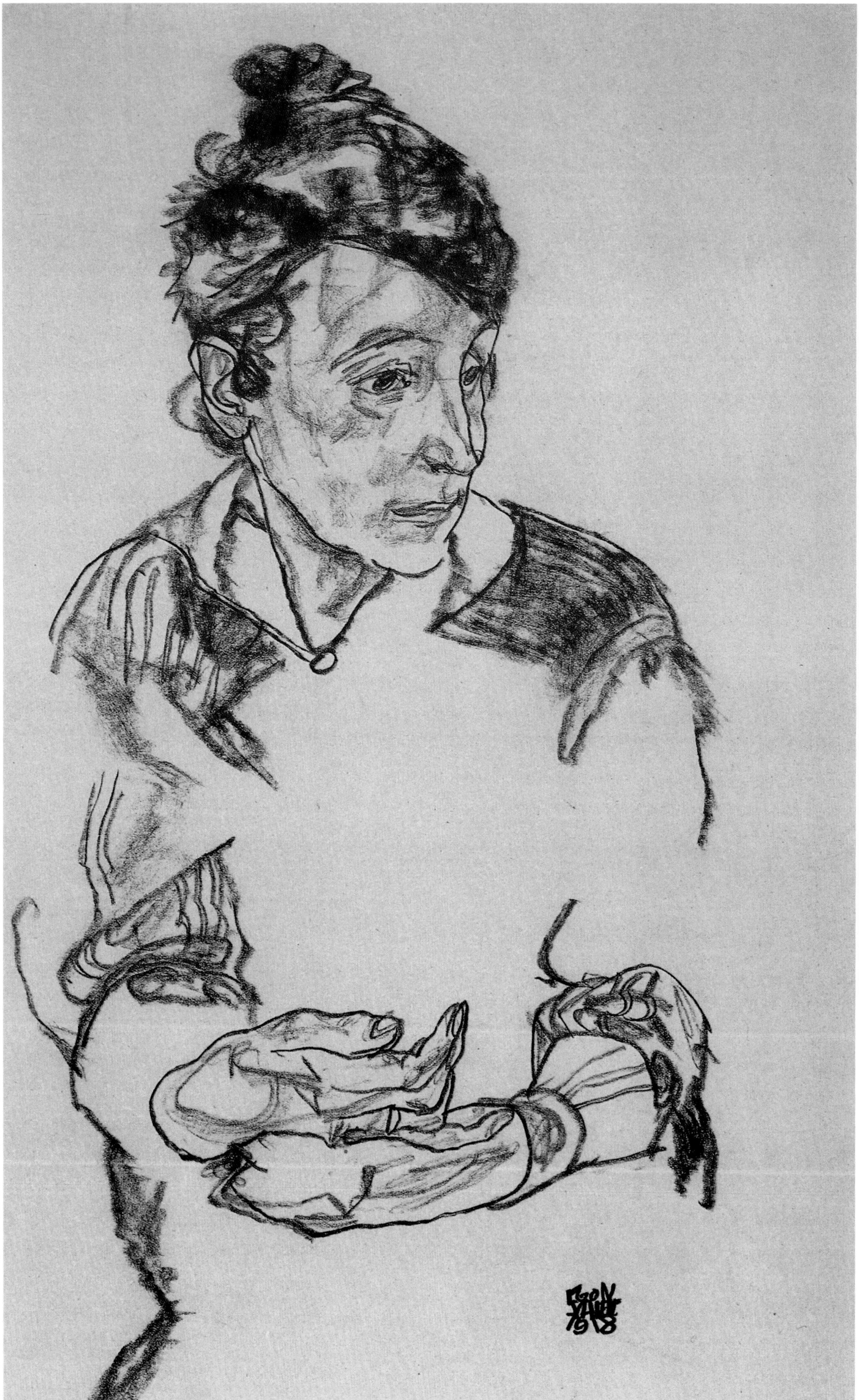

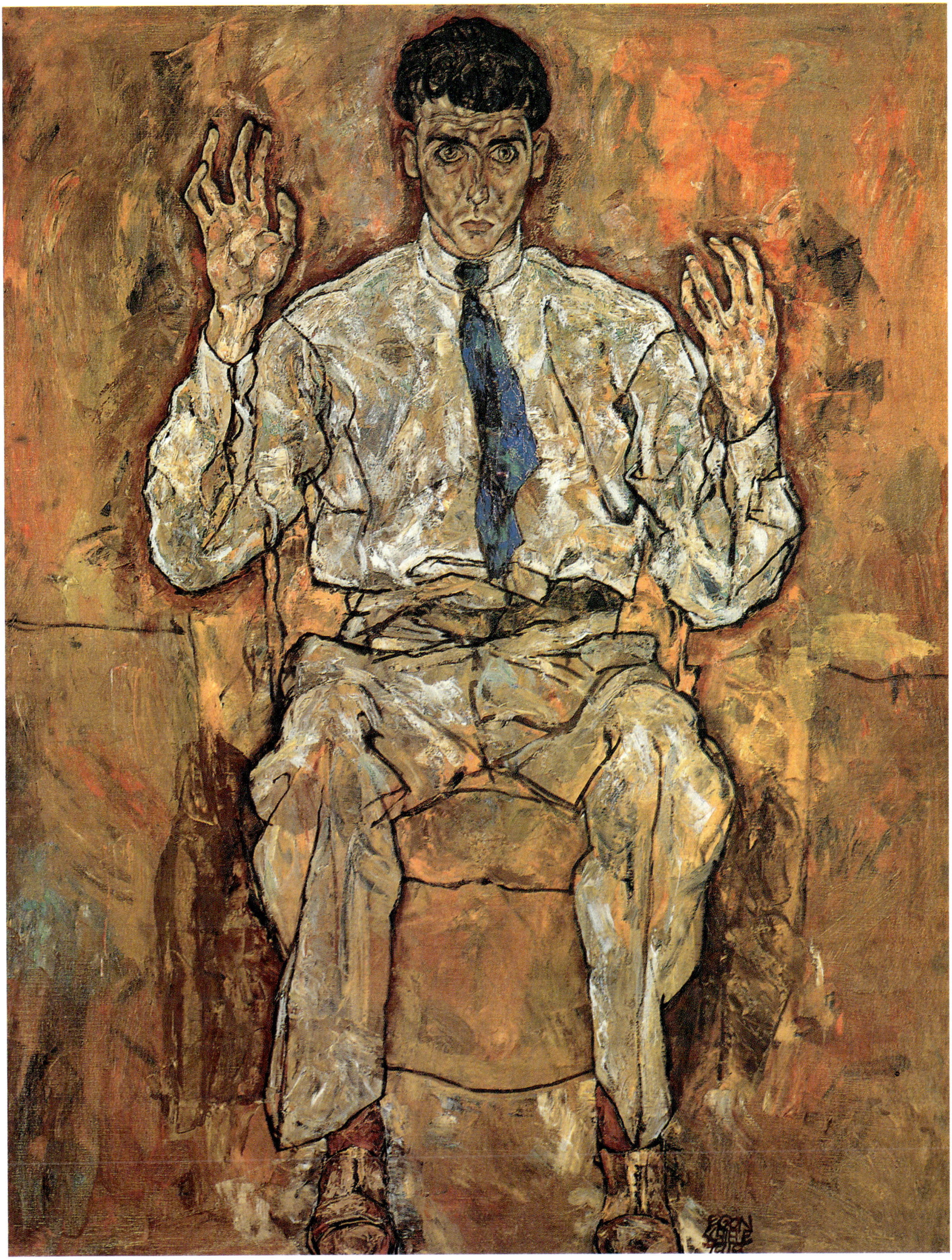

Left:
Portrait of Marie Schiele, 1918
Pencil and charcoal, 11½ × 7 inches (29.4 × 18 cm)
Graphische Sammlung Albertina, Vienna

Portrait of Albert Paris von Gütersloh, 1918
Oil on canvas, 55 × 43½ inches (140 × 110.4 cm)
The Minneapolis Institute of Arts, Minneapolis
Gift of P.D. McMillan Land Company

Right:
The Family, 1918
Oil on canvas, 59 × 59 inches (150 × 150 cm)
Österreichische Galerie, Vienna

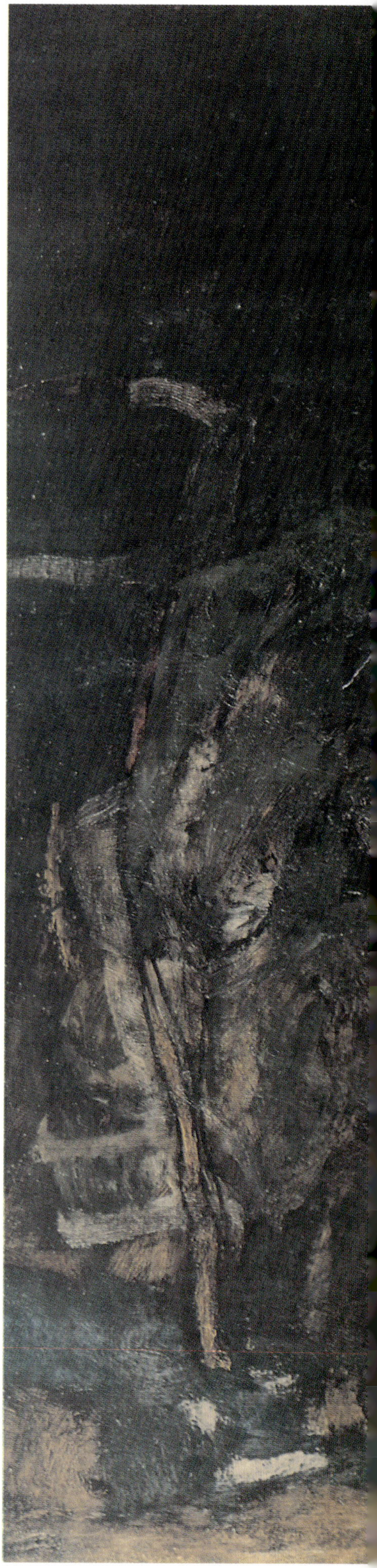

Page 42:
Secession Exhibition poster, 1918
Color lithograph
Graphische Sammlung Albertina, Vienna

Page 43:
Woman Sitting with Left Leg Drawn Up, 1918
Watercolor and pencil on gouache, 15 × 12 inches (46 × 30cm)
National Gallery, Prague

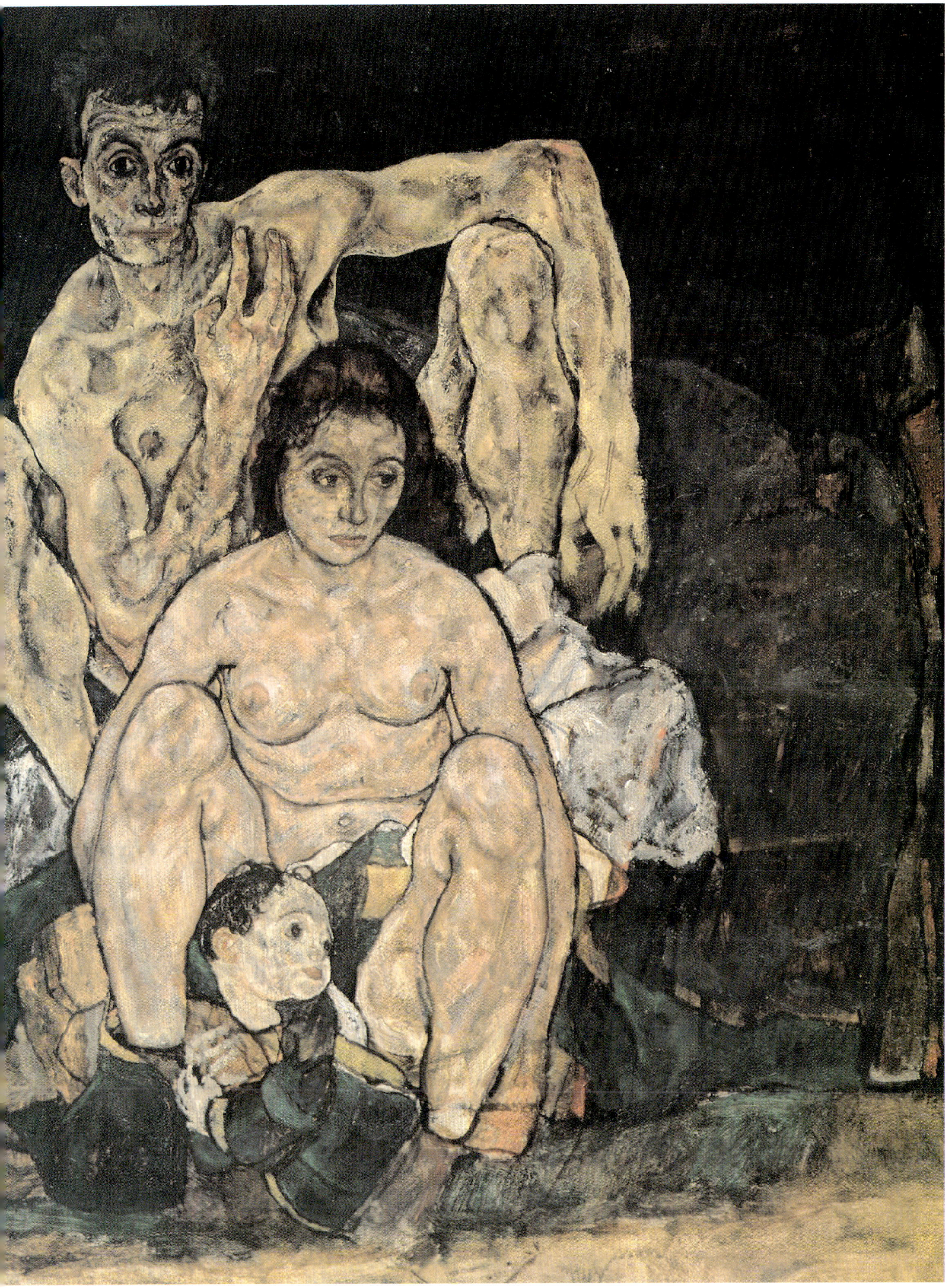

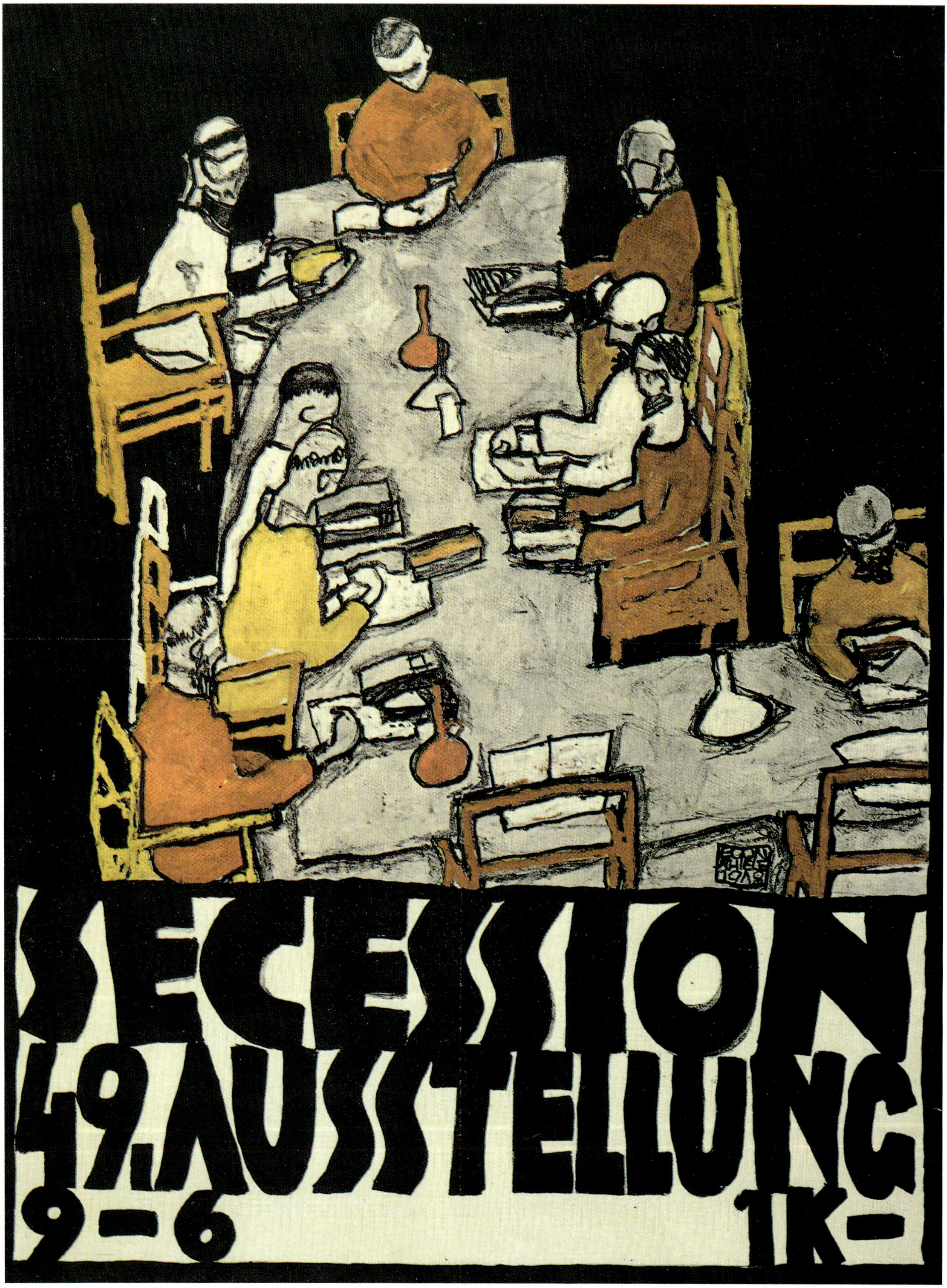
SECESSION
49. AUSSTELLUNG
9–6
1K–

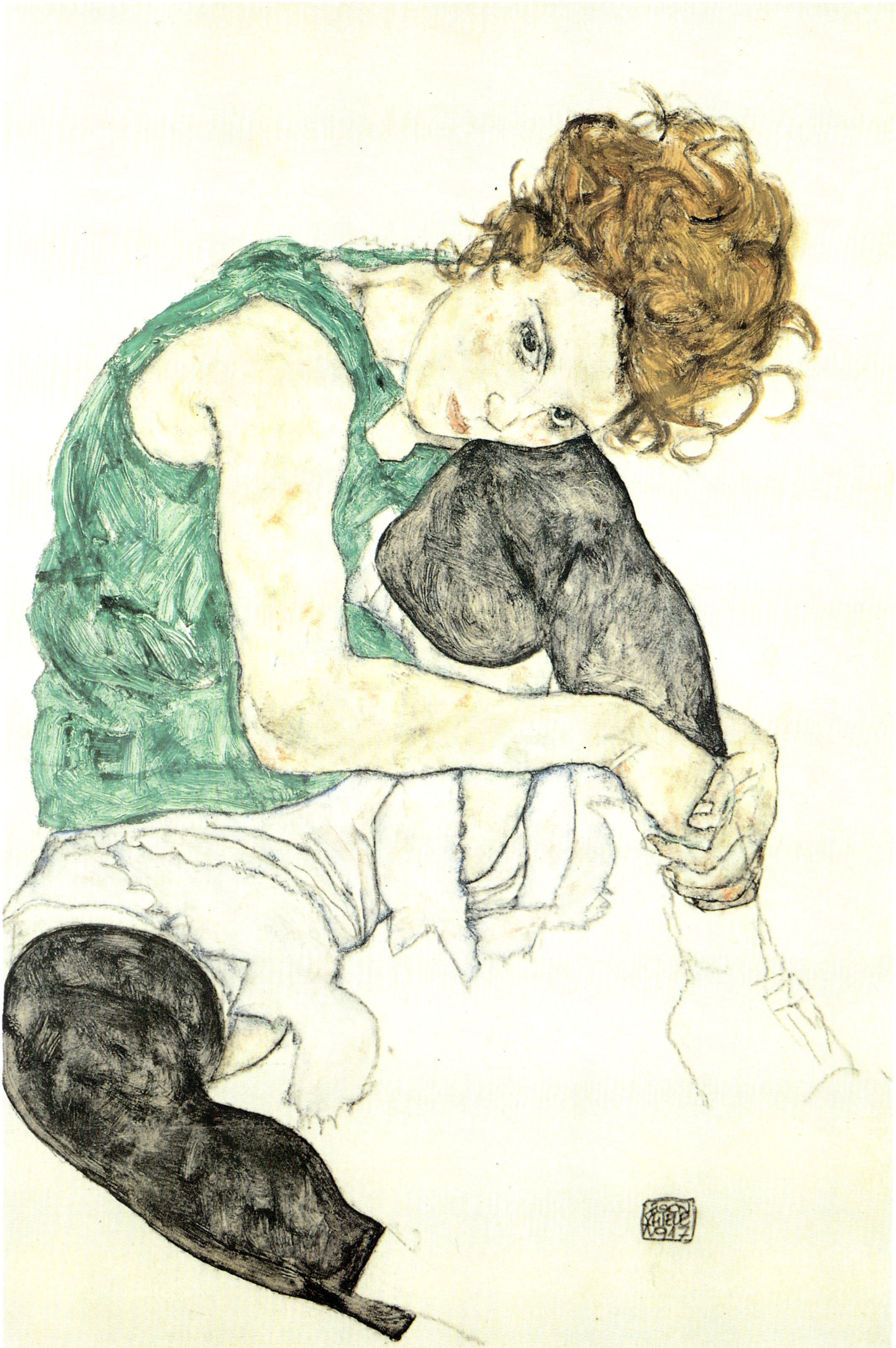

ACKNOWLEDGMENTS

The publisher wishes to thank Martin Bristow, who designed this book. The following provided illustrations:

Graphische Sammlung Albertina, Vienna: pages 12, 15, 16, 18, 22, 23, 28-29, 34, 38, 42
Haags Gemeentemuseum, The Hague: page 33
Historische Museum der Stadt Wien, Vienna: pages 17, 27
Kunsthaus, Zurich: page 13
The Minneapolis Institute of Arts: page 39 (Gift of the P.D. MacMillan Land Company)
National Gallery, Prague: page 43
Neue Galerie der Stadt, Graz: page 19
Neue Galerie am Landesmuseum Joanneum, Graz: pages 11, 35
Neue Pinakothek, Munich: pages 20-21
Niederösterreichisches Landesmuseum, Vienna: page 10
Öffentliche Kunstsammlung, Kunstmuseum, Basel: page 25
Österreichische Galerie, Vienna: pages 14, 30-31, 32, 36-37, 40-41
Private Collections: pages 24 (Photograph Galerie Im Griechenbeisl, Vienna), 26